MORALS AND MANNERS

FOR THE MILLENNIUM

Marilyn Gilbert Komechak, PhD

MORALS AND MANNERS
FOR THE MILLENNIUM

If you are unable to order this book from your local bookseller go to Amazon.com to download either as an e-book or a paper copy.

MORALS AND MANNERS FOR THE MILLENNIUM was first published in 2001 by Waltsan Publishing, Fort Worth, as a CD-ROM, a cdBook which included MP3 audio of the author reading the text. As the CD-ROM is no longer available from the publisher, the author has chosen to move the text on the disc to ebook and book print format.

*****

Credits

Formatting and cover design by Debora Lewis
www.arenapublishing.org

Cover photo courtesy Bigstock

*****

ISBN-13: 978-1480246256
ISBN-10: 1480246255

There is something that says morals and manners are waters of the same deep well—that manners spring from morals and are reflected on the face of society.

MARILYN GILBERT KOMECHAK, PhD

This book is dedicated to the many people whose names I do not know. You are the men, women, and young people who teach, comfort, care for, protect, rescue, preach, write, heal, and befriend. You are the people who give aid and hope to the rest of us. Among you are those whose names are my heart's connection: George, Gil, Matthew and Russel Komechak and Judie and Bill Silvers, and in memory of two heroes—

Russell Gilbert, my father who encouraged me to think for myself
and
John Kearney who raised not only his own children but mentored half the kids in west Texas.

Contents

ACKNOWLEDGMENTS

To Sandra Wellborn for her excellent editorial counsel. Like a fine physician, she knit together the bones of this book until it was strong enough to stand on its own.

Komechak, Marilyn G. "Questions in the Stardust Casino," Composers, Authors and Artists of America, Ed. Dr. Jeanne Hale, Vol., No. l, Winter, 308 Riverside Dr., New York, NY, 1994.

FOREWORD

There is resurgence in the air, something familiar yet decidedly new. As we catch our breath after that strenuous run through the gauntlet of the nineties, this newness carries the aura of having been given a second chance. As Spock said to Captain Kirk, "We've sustained some damage, but we are still able to maneuver."

Now is the time to correct our course, reassess missed opportunities, and calibrate our compass to true north. We are the people who are here, at this time, on our planet. We set the tone for the Millennium. This is our task, and this is our time. No wonder the air is filled with excitement.

This task is not unlike wearing a new pair of shoes—although they will have to be broken in, we know somehow they will carry us along on our journey into the future with more confidence.

In what follows, there will be many references to both factual and fictional literature. Although it's true that science gives us many things, it is art, literature, plays, and poetry to which we look for meaning.

Since one source of moral growth comes from reading, the vast literary terrain of meaningful books, poetry, art, and film will be a great resource for us. Through books, one's view of self and others changes. Art and books make us think. After that there is no turning back—unless it is away from ourselves. Through this we will discover, as poet Raymond Carver did, *A New Path to the Waterfall*.

As we mature, we become more open. The aperture of our perspective expands to allow in more light—more insight—and our focus wills us to build up rather than destroy.

It is as the actor Robin Williams replied when asked for his opinion about the present state of human affairs: "We can evolve."

SECTION I: MORALS

CHAPTER 1: THE MORAL INDEX

"The health of a community is an almost unfailing index of its morals."
—J. Martineau

The needle on a compass shows us where we stand and in what direction we face. But the question is, *where are we standing*? Some say we are knee-deep in a moral morass.

If the newspaper reports and television newscasts are any indication, we are in a deepening morality crisis. Novelist Barbara Kingsolver notes that children in this society have only two choices left—to be destroyed or to be destroyers. All other sane options have seemingly disappeared from their lives.

As I reflect on this state of affairs, I can't help but think about a book I was required to read for an undergraduate English literature course many years ago, *Lord of the Flies*. I recall how distasteful the reading of this little book was and the anxiety it provoked in me. I wanted done with it and the class discussions. I wanted to hurry along to something more pleasant.

Recently I was going over the book in my mind—comparing its text to modern- day events. That very day, I saw on the front page of our daily newspaper a picture and story about a teen who lives in our own neighborhood. Barrett, a high school senior, had just received the Wendy's High School Heisman Award, given each year to the outstanding student for academic and athletic excellence. Barrett and his family were flown to New York, and CNN covered the ceremony.

Feeling the need to understand the current social scene from a youthful perspective, I asked Barrett if I might read some of his winning essays. He agreed. To my surprise, he had cited the novel *The Lord of the Flies* to make a point about the current social and cultural state of affairs in the lives of young people. I had the feeling that he, too, saw this classic tale by William Golding very much as I did: an index finger pointing to what was to come.

In the years since its publication, a number of people, young and old, have noticed the way Golding's story presages our present time. It is as if he knew we would be facing a moral dilemma about now.

Lord of the Flies is a morality tale of human depravity in which Golding draws a graphic picture of the return to the savage side of human nature and what happens when human beings are released from the structure that supports society. The story focuses on a group of British schoolboys stranded on an island totally without adult supervision. Though at first it appears that all the boys will make a cooperative effort to work together, the situation rapidly goes "to the dogs." A boy named Ralph steps forward to take the lead, hoping to establish a kind of democratic law and order, but Jack, a boy with an antagonistic personality, challenges Ralph's leadership. Jack soon seduces the other boys into joining him in a hunt for wild pigs on the island. Bonding among the boys is consummated as they paint themselves like barbarians and go screaming like madmen through the jungle. Jack and his adolescent pals become destroyers in a full-blown moral meltdown. The result is mayhem: a miniature society on a rampage. Thus, the truth of how we treat others can be clearly seen at the place where morals and manners intersect.

But, returning to Barrett's essay, the young man gives several reasons why there should be rules for teens in our culture. In information gleaned from the Fort Worth police department's youth division, he learned that in 1998 more than 1,000 teenagers were fined a total of more than $200,000 for breaking the city curfew ordinance. Barrett feels that a curfew is necessary in our society as a tool which protects teens.

According to MADD (Mothers Against Drunk Driving), weekdays between 10 p.m. and 1 a.m., one in every 13 drivers is drunk. Barrett's research also revealed that between the early morning hours of 1 a.m. and 6 a.m. on weekends, the number of drunk drivers increases to one of every seven drivers. In single-vehicle fatal crashes in the US on weekend nights in 1994, 72.3 per cent of the fatally injured drivers were intoxicated (MADD, 1998 Summary of Statistics). In light of these statistics, it is clear that teens need to be protected from themselves. Curfews do keep teens off the streets and out of danger during times when accidents are most likely to occur.

"Graduated" Drivers. Most of the states are beginning to see the seriousness of the teen driving problem. Washington State's Senator Eide is sponsoring a bill proposing that after a teen gets a learner's permit at 15, an intermediate license must be *earned* at 16. *Time* columnist, Eugenie Allen, in a February 28, 2000, article, "Training Wheels," indicates that she feels Eide's proposed bill would save lives because *more practice* will mean fewer accidents in Washington State. Eide says, "This bill comes with a guarantee to save lives."

Senator Eide is particularly sensitive to the safety issues surrounding teen driving. Eide's own daughter, a responsible teenager, received a ticket two weeks after she became a licensed driver. Eide, a former hospital emergency room worker, had seen first- hand car wreck carnage involving inexperienced drivers. She is doing something about the basic problem: teens simply do not have enough experience to drive safely.

Help is On the Way. Allen's article outlines Eide's proposals for an intermediate license: "The Washington teen will not be able to drive between midnight and 5 a.m. unless the trip is necessary for school or work. There would be no passengers under age 21 except for family members. Intermediate drivers must log at least 50 hours of supervised driving, 10 of them at night. If they made it to the six-month mark with no moving traffic violations they can drive anytime with up to 3 passengers."

Allen's "Training Wheels" column cites additional data from AAA: "Some 6,000 teens will be killed in crashes of cars driven by teens; an additional 600,000 teens will be injured. Drunk driving is causing fewer accidents these days thanks to zero-tolerance laws and higher alcohol-purchase ages."

More information for setting up your own driving graduated-license program is available at www.driverzed.org and www.highwaysafety.org.

There are several other reasons why teenagers need guidelines, adult supervision, and limits. Barrett's article introduced earlier further states: "In our culture, we can see the horrors of what happens when people are left to their own devices without any guidelines. In 1996, there was a group of boys in Florida who started their own gang called "Lords of Chaos" (TV Documentary, February 1999). It is not known whether or not the boys patterned themselves after *Lord of the Flies*. But these initially innocent, harmless teenage boys started as friends out to have a good time. But because there was hardly any accountability, the kids turned to petty theft and eventually murder."

The documentary detailed how this band of boys murdered their high school teacher following a disagreement with him. People, particularly children, when left to their own devices, can live out their own horror stories.

Think about this: these children weren't considered to be "bad kids." They were accepted by other kids and adults and were seen as normal kids. Just teenagers "being boys." However, as "The Lords of Chaos," without any clear-cut values or boundaries, they fulfilled William Golding's prophecy in *Lord of the Flies*.

Where Have All the Heroes Gone? We only have to look at professional sports today to see the obvious about a number of American sports "heroes." Their lives demonstrate the obvious: when one is given everything, and permitted everything "it is hard to keep from being king when it is in you and in the situation," to quote Robert Frost.

Celebrities, too, often cannot control their behavior. They act like petty tyrants who throw themselves and their money around, having come to believe they are above rules and consequences. One has only to look at the outcome of their behavior to see that, sooner or later, tragedy follows.

I applaud anyone who can maintain their integrity and continue to develop character and spirit while managing fame and fortune. Money and celebrity are not bad in and of themselves, but it is how we handle them that tells the tale.

A Russian and an Englishman Speak. Russian novelist Solzhenitsyn, who won the Nobel Peace Prize in 1970, speaks through a character in his book *One Day in the Life of Ivan Denisovich* to tell us "the higher up the work camp chain of command, the more often one sees laziness, ineptness, and cruelty." And Lord Acton, an English historian and member of the House of Commons, said in 1887, "Power corrupts, but absolute power corrupts absolutely."

When we are granted privileges we have not honorably earned or when we are overcompensated for a job, the chances are we will lose control of the situation. Where there are no restraints on power, there can be no beneficial outcome. As great literature and reality have shown—in any environment that is without a moral code, anything can happen.

Young Girls. February 8, 2000, PBS ran a revealing TV documentary, *The Lost Children of Rockville County*. In it, we were given a glimpse into the social lives of a group of high school students in Conyers, Georgia, just 25 miles outside of Atlanta. Routine medical exams revealed an outbreak of syphilis among the teens. This documentary gave evidence again and again that these kids felt numb. They experienced no feelings of guilt, remorse, social conscience, loyalty, or love. They could not feel their own feelings, and a full 70 per cent of the students were sexually promiscuous. Yet these youngsters were well fed, clothed, and housed. They had all the material things but were without a sense of being connected to their families.

These upper middle-class boys and girls lived in well-manicured suburbs. My heart sank as I saw the girls give away their power to the boys, who took full advantage of the girls' passivity to degrade, use, and rob them of their inner beauty and joy of living. The girls seemed to be operating under the assumption that in order to be accepted by their peers, they had to join in the behavior of the most popular students in the school. The girls seemed helpless, almost robotic, as they met in secret with groups of boys and indulged the young males' every whim. The boys to whom the girls catered had sports cars, lots of spending money, and/or were popular members of athletic teams. In other words, the boys had "social status" in school. The boys were clearly in control and operated without limits or any kind of moral code. They engaged in all kinds of sexual perversion as a gang, with most of its members using some kind of dangerous "designer" drugs. The boys were aggressive in their approach to the girls and physically and emotionally abused them. As I watched the broadcast, I could see the girls' female spirits recoil as clearly as I could see their faces.

The group had even invited a known criminal—a drug dealer—into their mist. By doing so, they violated all the basic rules of their culture. This man truly became their *Lord of the Flies*. They naively looked to him as their protector. Consequently, in turn for his protection, he was to have his choice of the girls. Now we see the destroyers actually embracing someone who would, in turn, destroy them.

Before the PBS special, the parents knew nothing of their children's activities or lifestyles. Luckily, the documentary shocked some parents into awareness. The other parents who seemed to be unaffected by the broadcast, particularly the fathers of boys, managed to keep their "masculinity mask" in place. Just as in the "Lords of Chaos," the kids had just started out to have a good time. This documentary also clearly pointed out that the group of upper middle-class youths from Georgia could be from "Any town, USA."

Spinning the Chamber. I feel there is great damage being done to the mental and physical well-being of our country's young girls who seem to be playing Russian roulette with their bodies. Do they see themselves primarily as sex objects? Do they feel their worth and social status depends on whether or not they are some boy's girlfriend?

Many girls in high school and college date men who become controlling and abusive. Date rape is becoming more and more common. This *must* change. However, I believe that the social behavior of boys will not change without an outside influence. I predict that change *will* take place if the girls themselves become aware of the harm they are causing themselves. In addition, I believe that both boys and girls can benefit greatly if parents teach traditional values and help their children achieve self-respect. Self-respecting persons do not inflict damage on other people, even on those who, because of their social conditioning, assume subservient roles.

Disconnection and Disaffection. The core problem with many of our nation's youths is they are disconnected from their parents. The family rarely functions as a unit anymore. Kids are not, in truth, close to anyone. They may try desperately to connect with the "right kids" in school, and, if this doesn't happen, they go out of control. They are without bonds, except physical ones, to each other.

Often parents are very busy with their work and social lives. Most family counselors agree that a child has to know he or she is number one with his or her parents. Parents, indeed all of us, need to realize that any child is at risk of being lost if he feels his parents don't care about him.

During the 1960s I trained as a counselor. We studied the feeling of alienation that was rapidly becoming rampant in the world. We discussed the increasing amount of loneliness and estrangement that was being experienced in the lives of adults and children alike. The period of prosperity following World War II was taking its toll. The majority of families no longer consisted of a working father and a stay-at-home mother. In many homes, both parents worked, and in many cases, only one parent headed the family. There was less time available for the children for recreational or training purposes. The children themselves tried to create families of their peers and became "flower children." Teens left for cults every day. We still see some remnants of the hippie movement in the Haight-Ashbury in San Francisco. There are still flower children—only they are no longer passing out flowers.

No Shield. I suspect there is more than a grain of truth in what an elderly gentleman once told me: A man will protect a woman from everyone but himself. Girls need to learn at an early age how to identify male predators, regardless of how smooth talking the boy or man may be. Fathers, as well as mothers, can screen the boys their daughters date. They can help their daughters develop realistic criteria for differentiating the immature from those who will be able to develop friendships. This ability to evaluate people is a process that begins early in the life of girls.

Fathers in particular, even without a word, have a great influence on the kind of boys their daughters choose to date. If a father distances himself from his daughter, shows little interest in her, or criticizes her inordinately, she may "act out" to show her father that she *is* valued by other males. She may become promiscuous to prove to him that other males value her.

A daughter who has not felt validated by her father will make one of two choices. In a bid to gain what she's lacking—male approval and attention—she will become a doormat for any male who looks at her. Or she may date boys who are rebellious, wild, and openly hostile to her father or adult authority figures. This last choice will surely get her father's attention.

The daughter who can successfully evaluate the boys she dates is a girl who has been and continues to be *validated* by her father. He gives her the message that he likes and approves of her, and he is interested in her activities. They can talk and laugh together. He has taken part in setting a curfew with and for her and helps evaluate parties and activities in which she participates. He knows where she is and who she is with. She is aware she is accountable to her parents. Because she has worked with her parents to develop age-appropriate rules and structures, she is freer in make relationship decisions. In a culture in which "when the whistle blows any thing goes," she is apt to experience less social anxiety because she has structure, rules, and her parents' vigilance and support.

In such a relationship, the father will meet his daughter's date cordially and spend some time talking with him. In other words, the father has a chance to look the boy over (in psychology we call this the EBT, "eyeball test"). Later, in a relaxed conversation, the father can ask his daughter *her* impression of her date. She can ask her father what he thought of the young man, or he can offer his opinion in a friendly way. The girl will then have the value of her father's experience, his words, to build on in her future evaluations.

The Third Option. I live near a large high school and can see some of the behavior exhibited by the youth who go to that school. Shortly after school began one fall, I noticed a couple who, each day, would sit on the curb near our house and talk for what must have been their entire lunch period. The boy dragged furiously on a cigarette the whole time. In later months, they would walk up and down our street engaging in talk and playful behavior, the boy always sucking on a cigarette. I regret to report that, six months later, I saw the girl taking drags off the boy's cigarette. They no longer appeared to be so playful or so in love. It rather looked like the cigarette had gained their full devotion and was all that remained of their relationship.

So when a young man like Barrett comes along, it gives all of us more hope. He was able to decide that he didn't have to be either the destroyed or the destroyer. Barrett has clearly chosen a third option: to be a person of integrity. Let us develop in our children this sense of the third option!

Haley, Texas, 1959. A novel has appeared on the horizon that carries the same warning as Golding's book. A review written by Bob Reed appeared in the Sunday, January 16, 2000, issue of the Fort Worth Star-Telegram about the book *Haley Texas 1959* by author Donley Watt. The reviewer mentions what Watt calls the "watershed times of my youth."

The story doesn't take place on a desert island. It is not framed in the suburbs or in a large city. And while it is not as horrifying or as ghastly as *Lord of the Flies*, it warns again of malevolence on the loose. We have only to look at the news of what took place in Jasper, Texas, to see its form.

Just as in the other examples, the boys, restless, with nothing to do but take orders from their tough fathers, spend a great deal of time cutting and burning second growth mesquite in the pasture of the ranch. The reviewer says, "The boys just out looking for fun and excitement—or maybe to escape boredom—get together on a Saturday night. A game is thought up as they drive along the rural back roads in their truck."

"They keep an eye out for any lone person walking along the road. When one such person is spotted, a board is extended out of the truck, and the person, usually black, is knocked down as they pass."

Author Watt, reflecting on his youth, speaks about his own growing up: "A few critical events, measured only in moments, set off by parenthesis, nudge us this way or that, and we can never turn back. It was a brutal sport. I knew it at the time. I knew it was wrong, but I couldn't back out. Not then."

The protagonist, Donnie, has as a father a man who is stern and uncompromising. As happens during hard times when survival is in question, the father gives little thought to the boy's inner life and needs.

I think all of these stories and TV documentaries point up the importance of achieving a *balance* in raising children. We are either overindulging children and letting them run wild, or we discipline with the hand of a dictator in a way that is so harsh it stunts their emotional growth.

Raising boys. I am reminded of another book, *Real Boys*. The author, William S. Pollack, psychologist and coordinator of the Center for Men at McLean Hospital, Harvard Medical Center, studied sad, lonely, frustrated, and depressed boys. He makes a profound statement: "<u>Boys who can't cry will cry bullets</u>." We are seeing the awful truth in this statement in schools around the country. We see the very thing Pollack describes as a "boy code"—the unwritten creed that teaches boys to cover up their emotions. This "masculinity mask" creates boys who are at risk, and, at times, dangerously angry. Boys, who, in reality, are lonely and depressed.

In addition to the "boy code" of keeping silent even through hurting, Pollack identified another aspect of our culture harmful to boys: reinforcement for being tough. That is, they are encouraged to never let their "masculinity mask" slip. It is this covering up of emotions that is thought to bring about boys' irrational preoccupation with guns, a rising tendency to self-destruction, poorer scholastic performance than that of girls, and a drive toward dangerous delinquent behavior.

The "boy code" is furthered by the use of shaming techniques such as calling a boy a "wimp" or a "wuss." As one might surmise, this kind of shaming produces men who are divorced from their feelings and disconnected emotionally in their marriages.

Pollack maintains that the one saving event for a boy is to receive empathy—an empathy that is vigorous and lighthearted. (Empathy is the ability to genuinely feel and be sympathetic with what the other is feeling due to having been in the same or similar situation; put oneself in another person's place and objectively experience emotions from the other person's perspective.) Boys, Pollack's research substantiates, are starved for empathy. When this need is not met, the boy develops a kind of hidden malaise that is too often misread. Such boys become increasingly anxious and aggressive, and, although the boy is developing normally, he is wrongly labeled as having attention-deficit/ hyperactivity disorder (ADHD).

Who me? Men who as boys were indoctrinated in the "boy code" had felt disconnected and lonely. Consequently, as adults, they find they cannot tolerate or understand intimacy in relationships. Steven Carter's book *Men Who Can't Love* refers to these men as commitment phobics. It is my feeling that when a man does risk intimacy, the relationship can have a healing effect.

Personally, I do not feel that men, as a group, are all that fearful of being in committed relationships; research shows that most men thrive by being part of a couple. Valid studies have shown that when some men are widowed and remain single, they seem to lose a great deal of their vitality and health.

Fear of intimacy, brought on early in life by living the "boy code" and wearing the "masculinity mask," can create fear in the extreme. This fear can turn boys and men into sexual predators. When lacking any real self-confidence and emotional maturity, if the male is frustrated or loses face, he can become violent. Rape may well be a response to powerlessness . . . not the victim's but the perpetrator's. Rape is, after all, not about sex but about power.

Pollack sees many parents treating boys like "little men." He feels that boys in our culture are expected to separate from their mothers too soon. Showing fear is not acceptable behavior, and boys are responding to this command with bravado and outrageous behavior. When tyrannical coaches or teachers work with them, their development is likely to be further compromised.

Being tough with boys when they are starving for empathy drives their emotions underground. Pollack believes boys and men hide their feelings even from buddies and family, and, most of their lives, when asked how they feel will respond with "I'm fine."

In phrasing a question to a male, I believe it is best to avoid asking "How do you feel?" (about this or that) because often they do not know how they feel. Most men can answer a question when phrased "What do you *think?*" They can easily identify the feelings of anger or frustration but not their other feelings.

Pollack's revealing studies will surely help us as parents and the boys we live with. It is my hope that *Real Boys* will prompt as much concern about boys' emotional health as Mary Pipher's 1994 best seller *Reviving Ophelia*, has done for girls.

Learning Violence. Violence is modeled daily for our kids on television. And I am not referring to the slapstick comedy. I am sure you have noticed that killing on TV and in the movies is so commonplace that it has become a national form of entertainment. It continues to sluice into our nation's subconscious. We are not peaceful, and we have become, in my opinion, a restless and anxious nation. Can you wonder how our children feel? While reviewing a typical TV "fare," the message seems to be that violence pays—but it is society that will pay (and is paying) a very dear price for this kind of "entertainment." A child learns from almost all channels and at any time of the day or night that—when he or she gets mad or others do something he or she doesn't like—it is perfectly acceptable behavior to shoot them.

In Stephen Crane's 1895 novel *The Red Badge of Courage,* a picture is clearly drawn of those he calls "those little souls who thirst for fight." Crane was not only a novelist but also a war correspondent. He knew firsthand that a part of human nature thirsts for "blood news." Then, as today, the motto in the newsrooms of the nation is "If it bleeds, it leads."

What is this fascination with violence? Do we not know that by participating in violence even passively, we are drawing violence into our lives? In response to a real need, there are anger management clinics springing up all over the country. Many judges are referring people to these clinics.

I wrote the following song lyric as an expression of how I see many people reacting to our national moral crisis:

"Crayons and Guns"

Verse:　Kids pack crayons and guns to school
How can they learn what's wrong from right?
We're all barred, locked, and alarmed
Looking behind us day and night.

Chorus:　We're not free, we're not free
Fear is destroying democracy
We're not free, we're not free.
Will a bullet be our destiny?

Verse:　Child who's playing in her own yard
Is shot by some kids in a gang war.
Now the sun's spotted with blood
The enemy's living right next door.

Chorus:　We're not free, we're not free
Fear is destroying democracy
We're not free, we're not free
Will a bullet be our destiny?

Verse:　We've made peace with the Arab sheiks
And now we call the Russian friend
Yes it's time people like us
Bring this hatred to an end.

Chorus:　We're not free, we're not free
Fear is destroying democracy
We're not free, we're not free
Will a bullet be our destiny?

Early American educator Abraham Flexner voices his sentiments on parenthood: "Being a parent used to be one of the most simple, inevitable developments in the world. But nowadays, one has no business to be married unless, waking or sleeping, one is conscious of the responsibility." I have heard a counseling authority go so far as to say, "A couple ought to be given a test to see if they are capable of raising children before they are married."

Uninvolved Parents. Today, many child experts are worried that uninvolved parents are raising amoral children. As one can see by the TV documentaries, our nation's children are raising themselves. The least of our problems is that they are aimless and unanchored.

Fort Worth Star-Telegram writer Stephen G. Michaud in a December 22, 1995, interview with pediatrician Dr. Tom Rogers Jr. quotes the doctor: "We are raising our kids in a moral vacuum. Parents are cheating their children by not giving them what they need most: love and guidance and boundaries in their lives."

Dr. Rogers goes on to say: "The kids have lost their sense of home. They're far less confident of the future. Their attention spans have contracted. They're unhappy too, and that shows in their health. We have a lot of problems with emotional disease. Depression, suicide attempts. Eating disorders and drugs, obviously."

The alarm has been sounded. There is no longer any doubt that there are fewer and fewer adults, and subsequently, children, who are practicing basic moral values. Parents seem to fall into the two most prevalent extremes: physical abusers and those who are afraid their children won't like them if they discipline.

The "Brat" Syndrome. I know you've seen them too. They are everywhere: in the malls, restaurants, parks, movies, even churches. It is impossible to miss them. These kids are not welcome in stores because they drive other patrons away, handle all the merchandise, pull the toys off the shelves, create messes the employees have to clean up, and play with anything that catches their eye—often in such a destructive manner as to make the merchandise unsalable. Still the parents fail to discipline their behavior.

A frazzled parent feels compelled to make "her dear" a separate meal because the child says he doesn't like what was prepared for the rest of the family. Some of these kids are verging on malnourishment because they mainly eat foods heavy with sugar and starch rather than vegetables, fruits, and protein. Younger parents who grew up being given a lot of fatty, starchy, sugary foods by their overindulgent parents find it difficult to deny *their* children the "pleasure" of such treats. Thus they rationalize the overindulgence of *their* children. However, not only are the parents encouraging bratty behavior in their children, tooth decay and obesity are becoming more prevalent in children and adolescents.

Parents who don't discipline their children produce brats. When parents give in to the whining and begging, the child has learned how to work the "demand-and-get" angle. Parents of brats incorrectly think they must be friends with their children when, in fact, they need to be *friendly, but firm*. There is nothing wrong with a parent enjoying a child, being close and having fun together. In fact, it is highly advised. But parents of brats are not truly enjoying their children. Instead, their children are leaving footprints all over the parents. It is called being "walked on."

Get Up Off the Floor, Mom and Dad. Assert yourself. Hold the line. Do what you say you're going to do so that the kids come to believe that *what you say is what you mean*. Be someone your kids look up to. Remember, *you* are the authority—moral and otherwise—in your children's lives

Broken Moral Compasses. Psychologists understand that parents who have "broken moral compasses" are not going to provide their children with the "know-how" to map out and live in this complex world. Children absorb parental values and standards like a plant absorbs nutrients. If these values are "broken" or poisonous, the subsequent growth is warped and stunted. Consequently, these children may never find their place in the world. These are the runaways who are adrift, searching for "home."

How About Frustration? Children *must* experience frustration some of the time and at appropriate levels. Not to do so leaves them without the coping skills necessary for the tough times ahead of them. Children who have not learned coping skills are much more likely to commit suicide when they receive rejection or cannot have what they want. And, as we all know, life abounds with both of these frustrating situations.

However, a child who has navigated the waters of frustration and learned to deal with it—with appropriate mature adult guidance—is much more likely to come through intact. In fact, whenever the experience of hurt or disappointment comes, the child will eventually transform it into a growth experience.

A pampered child, on the other hand, one who has been made into a miniature queen or king, becomes a helpless person, unable to cope with tough times. These kids will stay emotionally immature into, and more than likely throughout, adulthood.

I Want It Now! If a parent is always there to give instant gratification, the child never learns to wait (i.e. the brat). Being able to wait is one of the prerequisites for adulthood. Some "grown-ups" we meet are still emotionally at age two and failing miserably at most of the aspects involved in mature adult life. Parents who pamper kids cripple them and rob them of their ability to face life and make something of themselves. They lack inner strength and may not thrive.

Tougher laws in Texas are demanding more accountability from offenders and their parents. These laws highlight the rights of society and have been a long time in coming. But even more importantly, these tough laws are helping shape kids into more emotionally intelligent and resilient individuals. What do I mean by that? These laws help teach children how to extend empathy, tolerance, generosity, and compassion to another person *and to themselves* when needed. Sentencing a youngster in trouble to community service is but one of the ways this is being accomplished. Kids catch on quickly when there are immediate consequences for destructive actions in combination with a structure for communicating productive behaviors.

It's About Waiting. In psychologist Daniel Goleman's book, *Emotional Intelligence*, he cites studies done with four-year-olds at Stanford University. One remarkable study tested a child's ability to delay gratification, or, in other words, impulse control. In the study, the children were offered the choice of enjoying a single marshmallow immediately (immediate gratification) or two marshmallows (impulse control) when the tester returned from an errand. The results were not surprising. Years later, when the same set of youngsters took their Scholastic Aptitude Test, Goleman reports those who had the self-discipline to wait for two marshmallows outscored the more impulsive subjects by an average of 210 points.

Detoxing Our Society. Children absorb the emotional toxins in our world by osmosis. Elizabeth Dole, former head of the Red Cross, has stated, "Violence and obscenity have become prerequisites for entertaining us. Our popular culture coarsens our souls in so many cases." She goes on to say, "Our children are suffering from a daily assault by a toxic culture, a culture focused on violence and incivility that's poisoning their spirits and undermining generations of solid values."

Just Say "No" to TV. Early on in my children's lives, I monitored their TV viewing. I had received a list of those TV programs appropriate for their age level and a list of those that were not. Of course, this brought on much protestation because "None of our friends' parents do that!"

Last week, I looked to see what was being offered on the "TV menu" that day. I had a little "downtime" and wanted to watch a program or two just to unwind. The assortment of programs offered between 7 p.m. and 12:30 a.m. included stories about how people got out of a traffic ticket; a show called *Greed*, a show about actual people behaving with destructive and violent behavior; a hostile group discussing how relatives have slighted them; murder at a publishing house; two children discovering their parents had been lying to them; information on how to start an escort service; and a man who had fathered two children by two women talking about his broken engagement and dishonest son. Well, enough. I've made my point.

Today, however, my spirits rose somewhat as I saw this sage advice in William Dyer's book, <u>The Wisdom of the Ages</u>. "We must wake up and look at what we are teaching! Instead, let us teach empathy, that experience of feeling, to a degree, what another person is experiencing."

This is very important, because, to my way of thinking, empathy is a younger form of mercy. If we give ourselves empathy and we can then give it to others, mercy will follow.

Mercy is a quality which William Shakespeare said, "becomes the throned monarch better than his throne." This quote applies equally to those of us without crowns. Knowing the meaning of and being willing to give mercy is a gift—both to the recipient and to the receiver. Shakespeare calls this gift a "double blessing."

In detoxing our society for our children, and our adult selves, we can promote those companies and individuals that do not sponsor violence and/or pornography. Another avenue is to utilize chips already being installed in select televisions and program-controlled internet access software to control the programming that comes into our homes.

Consider supporting The Parents' Television Council, P.O. Box 7802, Burbank, CA 91510-9817. Steve Allen is the honorary chairman. You may have seen their ad in many newspapers across the nation. This is a group of people concerned about those TV programs that have become very much like moral sewers, and the negative impact the programs are having on our children. (On a personal note, I must confess Steve Allen and Carol Burnett are my favorite comedians of all time. I have only seen them do wholesome, quality humor.)

<u>What Does the Public Think About All This</u>? Guest columnist Lee Cullum, in the June 30, 1997 issue of the Dallas Morning News, referenced a survey conducted in 1997 by Public Agenda. The Americans surveyed remain deeply troubled by the nation's youth whom they felt were "rude, irresponsible and wild."

"It seems like kids are more destructive now," observed a man from Denver. "There is an anger inside them."

The survey also reveals the feeling that, "parents are so lacking in time, so hurried and consumed by financial burdens and acquisitions, they are giving the children things instead of themselves. They've shunned being the moral authority and, thus, children are becoming mindlessly acquisitive mini-consumers who demand—and get—electronic gadgets, designer clothes, and sneakers, things they have come to expect as a matter of right."

Afraid to Discipline. There are parents who fear to discipline their children, or may be afraid the child will report them to the authorities. On the other hand, some parents are engaged in physically abusing their children and killing their spirits. Such extremes!

As discussed earlier, the children of those parents who are afraid to discipline are clearly in control of the adults. The kids are boss. They call the shots. And that deserted island is looming on the horizon.

Lee Cullum concluded that the survey respondents believe that moral guidance is what the children are missing. Cullum says, "Moreover, couples are spending long hours at the office because they want to escape the hard work at home." The conclusion is worrisome. Children are rearing themselves.

However, as I heard one savvy father warn his adolescent son (the boy having done "something really stupid"), "*What you are doing now, you are becoming.*" That must have jarred something awake in the young man. He began to change his shiftless behavior, stopped blaming everyone else in the family for his lack of good fortune, and went out and got a job.

Value Inoculations. To find a healthy young man in this toxic culture was, for me, quite heartening. It is true then, that young people like Barrett *can* surface at the end of high school, alive and well. Barrett is first to acknowledge his parents' role in his phenomenal success. Parents who were there, who cared, who disciplined, provided moral guidance, and modeled for him how to be a successful human being, in the true meaning of the word. But, remember it was Barrett who ultimately was the one who made the hard choices that are leading him to a bright future.

No Ostrich This One. Barrett has not had his head in the sand. He strikes me as being both aware of and yet inoculated against the poison of our times; protected by his values, instilled by a family which lives their values. When he will experience hard times in his life (and they do come to us all), he will be able to rebound, and make his way forward. This young man is committed in all his actions and words to finding a better way.

Designing a Supportive Social Milieu. In the summer of 1995, Crosspoint, the counseling center, at the St. Matthew's Episcopal Cathedral in Dallas, was publishing a newsletter. I was asked to answer a question sent to the "Ask the Doctor" column. The question asked: "How can I raise my child to be a moral person?" This was my response:

*Let your own life exemplify those values you would want your child to adopt as his own. You will find this works better than stern lectures or a lot of "you shoulds." Those approaches tend to increase rebelliousness.

*Train in truth-telling. Punishing lies will have a rebound effect. The child learns to become cleverer in evading the truth. They come to realize very quickly that telling the truth gets them punished. Consequently when they are truthful say, "Thank you for being truthful. It shows you are honest. The rule you broke has the same consequences that we talked about before." (If you know a child has taken something, say, "I know you took the toy." Don't ask if he or she has taken it. If you do that, you are setting-up the child to lie.) Above all, be truthful yourself. And if at all possible, keep your promises. This builds trust between parent and child without which there can be no real relationship.

*Help your child learn to wait, that is, to be able to delay gratification for what he or she wants. As children get a little older, it is good for them to say what it is they want. Then you can talk with them about the obstacles to their getting it. Develop a plan to deal with those obstacles. Let them know how you, yourself, have gotten things by learning to wait and by having a plan.

*Teach your child the difference between assumed guilt and real guilt. Sometimes children blame themselves (assumed guilt) when things don't go right in their families. At other times they may try to avoid real guilt. It is important to teach the difference.

*When your child comes to you with a moral question, you can say, "I want you to think about that for awhile before I answer." (Then give them time to think.) Afterwards say, "What will happen if you do that (or don't do that?") This process helps children begin to learn independent thinking and decision-making and to prepare for the consequences of what they do. Those children who can evaluate situations, and who can think for themselves, are rarely found in religious cults.

So we see that children who are treated with respect, who trust their parents and experience consistent and appropriate consequences for their behavior, are much more likely to build solid personal morals.

Truth telling leads to empathy. This is a link that is rarely made, but inevitably, these same children, who have been trained in truth telling, will come to have an empathy with and an understanding of others – even for others who are different. It has been said that those who risk their own life to save others, in the moment of acting, feel full empathy with the other person. This is because they know what it feels like to be that other person. We often see empathy modeled in the acts of firefighters, policemen, doctors, nurses and paramedics, and others who give aid.

The Big Question. When Barry McCaffery, a West Point graduate and Vietnam veteran, took the job as head of ONDCP (Office of National Drug Control Policy) he, at first, wanted no part of it. He was about to turn down the President's appointment when his father asked him a question: "Do you think you can make a difference?" McCaffery said "yes" to his father's question and subsequently, "yes" to the job. I quote him here because I think he is very much on target with what we as Americans can do about the horrible destruction drugs wreak in the lives of the children of this country.

Call Off the War. McCaffery, (Director, Office of National Drug Control Policy) interviewed by Parade Magazine's Lisa Winik (January 16, 2000,) said he did not believe in a "war" on drugs. He tells parents that if they suspect a problem to, "Maintain your principles and don't go into denial."

McCaffery lets us know that those who *still have and have had* the most influences over drug behavior are families, mentors and communities. I list, with some abbreviation, his list of "Ten Ways to Drug-Proof Your Child."

1) Set a family standard on drug and alcohol use. Repeat it often. Live by it yourself.

2) Let kids know there are consequences and punishments for violating all family rules, such as no car or TV. Make the rules clear and fair, and enforce them.

3) Set aside time every day to talk with your kids about their lives, how they feel, what they think. LISTEN and care.

4) Help your children establish realistic personal goals. Encourage and help them to achieve their goals.

5) Know your children's friends and spend time with them.

6) Get excited about the things your kids care about. Do fun things as a family.

7) Be aware. Find out the warning signs of drug abuse, from physical changes to hostility to loss of interest in school or hobbies and watch for them.

8) Talk with your children about the future. Discuss responsibilities—yours and theirs.

9) Enjoy your kids. Make your home a happy, positive place.

10) Be a nosy parent. Ask your children questions; know where they are and with whom. Let them know you ask because you love them. (Barrett, the High School Heisman Award winner, said his mother believes it is her job not only to "expect," but also to "inspect." Wise mother!)

General McCaffrey goes on to say, "If you suspect a problem, search the Internet, call the drug clearinghouse, go to sources of strength like doctors and clergy. Otherwise, you will be leaving the problem up to law enforcement and emergency room physicians who will be dealing with your child or loved one.

Tips on How to Talk to Your Teenagers. Really *listen* to what your child is saying. This may be the hardest thing a parent does. Keeping silent is not really the same as listening. It is important that you track the child, stay with him and ask for clarification if you don't understand.

Think about disagreements as opportunities to identify and solve problems. Your adolescent does not think as you do. He or she does not have your experience or skills. In addition, no two people see a situation the same way. It is good to remember that if you were born in the child's body, had lived through the same time frame and had the same experiences, you, too, would be behaving in much the same way!

As a parent, if you think back to your childhood, you can recall how you reacted to your parents. You must also consider that some influences affecting your child's life just weren't there during your childhood. This may help you better understand what life is like for your teenager. Ultimately, you will be able to communicate better with your teen.

Two consulting PhD psychologists, Jane Brownstone and Carol Dye who worked in the seventies at St. Vincent's Hospital in St. Louis, Missouri, conducted workshops to help parents communicate with their teens. They asked parents to follow some simple rules of communication when talking to their children : to be aware of their voice tone and manner as much as their words, to avoid nagging and arguing; to stay calm and be courteous—no interrupting, and no name-calling or insults. When we as parents fail to follow these simple rules of communication, our children's only recourse is to defend their dignity and their perspective. Remember, we are modeling for them how to connect with another person, so we all come out winners! Try not to be judgmental or critical. Give your thoughts and ideas and tell your children *why* you hold the opinion you do. *Ask their opinion*. Find out how they feel.

Here is where empathy enters the picture. By putting yourself in your child' shoes, you become his advocate, allowing him to feel safe in the sharing of thoughts and feelings.

Mistakes can also become learning experiences. If the parent consistently does what he has said will be done, the child will come to value the parent's words. The child will actually listen. The child will hear the parent. If the child hears the parent say, "If you abuse the privilege of using the car, it will not be yours to use tomorrow," he or she knows those consequences will come to pass.

What the parent says is what the parent means. The consequences for breaking the rules will be predictable, and the parent will be seen, not as a mean authority figure, but as a reliable source. The child will come under control of his parent's words, and the parent will be believed.

But What Do I Tell My Dad? In my private practice as a psychologist, I had much better success teaching teenagers to communicate with their parents than I had teaching parents to communicate with their teens. The parents had to unlearn years of poor communication skills, and too often gave into anger and threats to control their children. However, even the least change, the smallest improvement in the parent's skills, particularly if they learned to listen better, brought about good results.

A Message fromThoreau and Dillard. I especially like what two essayists say to us about living life and about raising children. Henry David Thoreau sent us a message from his cabin on Walden Pond. In essence, he tells us if we are going to be fully alive, each morning as we awake we must know the rising sun is but a morning star. In that same vein, Annie Dillard, author of Living by Fiction, feels strongly that in the final analysis, we only teach our children what our parents taught us—to **wake up**.

Chapter 1 References

Allen, Eugenie, "Training Wheels," Time magazine, Feb. 28, N.Y., N.Y., 2000.

Crane, Stephen, The Red Badge of Courage, Appleton-Century-Crofts, NY, NY, 1992.

Cullum, Lee, "Survey shows adults' pessimism about nation's youth," Viewpoints, June 30, Star-Telegram, Fort Worth, Texas, 1997.

Golding, William, Lord of the Flies, Penquin Books, N.Y., August 1997.

Brandon, Barrett Elliot, "Teen Curfews: Are They Effective and Necessary, " Essay for Elks State Essay Contest, February 20, 1999, Fort Worth, Texas

Watt, Donley, Haley, Texas 1959, Reviewed by Bob Reed, Star-Telegram, Fort Worth, Texas, January 16, 2000, Novellas, Cinco Puntos Press, El Paso, Texas, 1999.

Michaud, Stephen G., Star-Telegram, "Uninvolved parents raising amoral children," December 24, Fort Worth, Texas, 1995.

Pipher, Mary, Reviving Ophelia, Putnam, NY, NY, 1999.

Pollack, William S. Real Boys, Random House, NY, NY, 1999.

Carter, Steven and Julia Sokol, Men Who Can't Love, M. Evans and Company, NY, NY, 1987.

Goleman, Daniel, Emotional Intelligence, Bantam Books, NY, NY, 1997.

Komechak, Marilyn Gilbert, Ask the Doctor, a column, "How to Raise a Moral Child," Crosspoint Counseling and Education Center, St. Matthew's Cathedral, Dallas, Texas, Vol. 2, Issue 1, Summer 1995.

Winik, Lisa, Parade Magazine, "He's Got A Better Way, Interview with General Barry McCaffrey, January 16, 2000, Parade Publications, 711 Third Ave., NY, NY.

Brownstone, Jane E. and Carol J. Dye, Communication Workshop for Parents of Adolescents, Research Press, Champaign, Illinois, 1973.

Dillard, Annie, Living by Fiction, Harper and Row, NY, NY 1982.

Thoreau, Henry David, "Where I Lived, and What I Lived For," in Masters of American Literature, Eds. Johnson, Paul and Simpson, The Riverside Press, Cambridge, Massachusetts, 1959.

Dyer, William, The Wisdom of the Ages, Harper Collins, NY, NY, 1998.

CHAPTER 2: POLITICS, MORAL CONSCIENCE AND SOCIAL JUSTICE

Poetry comes nearer the truth than history. —Plato
America is hard to see. —Robert Frost

It was George Washington who said, "I hope I shall always possess firmness and virtue enough to maintain what I consider the most enviable of all titles, the character of an Honest Man."

What are the qualities we should look for in those who are candidates for public office? It is important for political candidates to have demonstrated leadership, vision, administrative skills, and a passion for social justice. But above all else, the essential quality to look for in a candidate is *character*.

In Greek, the root word for character is engraving. A person with character is engraved—marked—by their journey through life. We see these engravings as patterns of personality. Habits that are followed long enough become part of one's character. And character, I believe, helps determine the quality—and outcome—of a life. The character of a United States President greatly impacts not only his life, but also the life of the nation. Character strongly influences the course of future events.

Consequently, to become politically responsible we must look at a candidate's credibility history. Is honesty a part of the engraved character pattern? If not, it should be.

Other things to consider when assessing candidates for government offices today: How many of life's challenges has the candidate met and mastered? How have they responded when dealt a hard blow by life? Can they be believed? If asked, what would they list on an inventory of their moral successes?

Honesty stands out as the one best indicator of character. Abraham Lincoln is "engraved" in our memory as "Honest Abe".

We also had a not-so-honest "Tricky Dickey". Unfortunately, Lyndon Johnson, a possessor of so many great qualities, was known on campus as "BS" Johnson. As President, his messages of hope and promise during the war in Vietnam deceived a nation, a psychic wound we are still trying to heal. As a nation we are starting to wise-up. It is, and will continue to be important to look at each candidate's credibility.

I am sure many fine individuals enter into politics with a true desire to accomplish what is best for the country and for their constituents. But our nation mistrusts public officials. I received the following message on the Internet and could not verify its source or veracity, but I believe it explains why we mistrust our public officials. Whether the following tally is true or false will be up to you to decide. The forwarded message began:

"And Are You Surprised?"

"Can you imagine working at the following company? It has a little over 500 employees with the following statistics:

*29 have been accused of spousal abuse
*7 have been arrested for fraud
*19 have been accused of writing bad checks
*117 have bankrupted at least two businesses
*3 have been arrested for assault
*71 cannot get a credit card due to bad credit
*14 have been arrested on drug-related charges
*8 have been arrested for shoplifting
*21 are current defendants in lawsuits
*84 in 1998 alone, were stopped for drunk driving
Can you guess which organization this is? Give up?

It's the 535 members of your United States Congress. The same group that perpetually cranks out hundreds upon hundred of new laws designed to keep the rest of us in line."

We will probably never know for sure if the political figures in the early days of this country committed a greater or lesser number of moral indiscretions. Yet, we can look back and discuss several people who had character and served our country well. Eleanor Roosevelt, for example, exemplified excellent personal and public qualities. She was called, "the best that America could be," and continues to be a model for people in government.

Our Better Angel. Let's look for a moment at the way in which Abraham Lincoln governed. Although under tremendous pressure while leading a country that was slaughtering itself in a civil war, he kept his wits and his conscience. During those most difficult of times, he found in himself what he had desperately wanted all Americans to find, and that was "our better angel." Lincoln hung his hopes on Americans finding within themselves what was good and true—their higher selves—at a time when the country was contemplating the evil face of war.

Horace Greeley, an American journalist and statesman, after all his editorials and orations chanting for war, had an about face. He nearly panicked after one defeat at the battle of Bullrun, and raised his voice for an armistice. But stoic Lincoln, like a scrawny horse hitched to a too-heavy plow, moved slowly forward with his principles.

Quilt Scraps. Lincoln had an enormous plodding patience as if he was somehow immune to the madness that was stalking through the streets near the capitol. The specter of a pending war frightened everyone as it roiled across the land. But Lincoln held the bleeding shreds of the fragmented country together; knowing that in the end, only a *union* would be able to survive. In his hands he smoothed each scrap, each thread. Although mournful, he felt if he could somehow keep the pieces cradled within his hands, those same remnants could later be stitched together into a strong, well-bound design that would become a true union.

People of our time still recognize Lincoln for his moral character. As recently as December 31, 1999, Time magazine's writer Paul Gray, proclaimed Lincoln as the "Conscience of the Century." When Lincoln signed the Emancipation Proclamation in 1863, he ended slavery. He also liberated the nation to begin living its ideals of democracy and freedom.

Many people have been inspired to live better lives because of the example set by Lincoln. I wonder if Davy Crockett's motto: "Be sure you're right, then go ahead," came from what he knew about Lincoln.

Yes, it was a simple honest politician who saved us from ourselves. He was able to accomplish what he did because moral courage had been ingrained in every fiber of his being.

Frontier Stoic. Lincoln grew up in Kentucky and Indiana. His parents, although poor, must have instilled in him grit, clear thinking and a tremendous generosity of spirit. Frontier life forged a great leader. Early in his career, he voiced his concerns about the state of the nation when he stated, "The sin of slavery is shared by North and South and it will have to be fought out on the battle fields. If God wills that it continue…until every drop of blood drawn with the lash shall be paid by another drawn with the sword."

Some time ago this list of *10 Cannots* found its way to my desk. Impressed by its ring of truth, I have kept it for these many years.

10 CANNOTS
By Abraham Lincoln

1. You cannot bring about prosperity by discouraging thrift.
2. You cannot help small men by tearing down big men.
3. You cannot strengthen the weak by weakening the strong.
4. You cannot lift the wage earner by pulling down the wage payer.
5. You cannot help the poor man by destroying the rich man.
6. You cannot keep out of trouble by spending more than your income.
7. You cannot further the brotherhood of man by inciting class hatred.
8. You cannot establish security on borrowed money.
9. You cannot build character and courage by taking away men's initiative and independence.
10. You cannot help men permanently by doing for them what they could and should do for themselves.

Yet, for all his practicality and serious demeanor, Abraham Lincoln was a lover of poetry. His speeches were filled with beautiful and great verse. He himself wrote three poems. One is "My Childhood Home I See Again," penned on a return trip to southern Indiana to campaign for Henry Clay. Southern Indiana was where he grew up and where his mother and sister are buried.

The entire poem consists of three parts. Following is part I of the poem.

My Childhood Home I See Again

My childhood's home I see again,
And sadden with the view;
And still, as memory crowds my brain,
There's pleasure in it too.

O Memory! thou midway world
'Twixt earth and paradise,
Where things decayed and loved ones lost
In dreamy shadows rise,

And, freed from all that's earthly vile,
Seem hallowed, pure, and bright,
Like scenes in some enchanted isle
All bathed in liquid light.

As dusky mountains please the eye
When twilight chases day;
As bugle-tones that, passing by,
In distance die away;

As leaving some grand waterfall,
We, lingering, list its roar—
So memory will hallow all
We've known, but know no more.

Near twenty years have passed away
Since here I bid farewell
To woods and fields, and scenes of play,
And playmates loved so well.

Where many were, but few remain
Of old familiar things;

But seeing them, to mind again
The lost and absent brings.

The friends I left that parting day,
How changed, as time has sped!
Young childhood grown, strong manhood gray,
And half of all are dead.

I hear the loved survivors tell
How naught from death could save,
Till every sound appears a knell,
And every spot a grave.

I range the fields with pensive tread,
And pace the hollow rooms,
And feel (companion of the dead)
I'm living in the tombs.

In this poem, you come close to the heart of the man as he writes about those people he knew in his childhood. It is evident they were on his heart. We see in him a man of tremendous moral courage and conscience—two great qualities of character for any person who seeks public office, or otherwise.

We Need to Know. In reflecting on the qualities that make a great leader, I was drawn to Gayle Sheehey's book, Character: America's Search for Leadership. Gayle is a social researcher of some credibility. In my mind, she provided a much-needed public service. She gave us an understanding of the personality dynamics of the person seeking office.

The book was written before the 1996 presidential election—and provided an historical and psychological profile of the candidates. I found her information insightful. She presented the profiles of Al Gore, George Bush, Bob Dole, and Ronald Reagan, to name a few. That she would spend a year of her life writing a book with such a short shelf life is one indication that she felt the public's need for such a book. I, for one, wish she would produce one for every presidential election. Her books would become as indispensable as the Voters' Guide. After all, isn't it wise to know the psychological bent of your public officials? Let's elect, on purpose, a man or woman of character!

Speaking of the Voters' Guide—We need to give a long delayed word of thanks to Mrs. Burns from Tennessee. She was a woman of character, and it is due to her that we, the "other half" of the population, now have the right to vote. She used her influence wisely, as you will see in the following account:

The Real Story.—By the summer of 1920, the battle over women's suffrage had been waging for nearly 75 years. President Wilson could no longer withstand the pressure and called a special session of Congress to address women's suffrage. At the beginning of the session, the majority of congressmen sympathized with the suffragists. As the bitter struggle between the two sides wore on, the suffragists saw their lead slipping. When the ballot was taken on August 18, a tie-vote was declared. However, the tie was broken in favor of suffrage by a congressman who had been expected to vote against suffrage—a 24-year-old legislator from the mountains of Tennessee by the name of Harry Burns. Just before he placed his vote, he found a note from his elderly mother in his pocket, reminding him " not to forget the ladies when you cast your vote." Later, when Harry was asked why had he changed his vote, he replied that it was a mother's job to give good advice to her children, and that his mother would not have given him bad advice.

Ms. Burns understood the importance of the moment, not only in the development of her son's character and what he could contribute, but also with respect to how the important decisions being made at the time would impact all people, especially women. Women can and do have a great opportunity to influence their children, and our world for good. But often it is only after a protracted struggle, as we see in the following situation. Hounds to the Fox, or, more appropriately, like a pack of wolves, they came. I refer to Eleanor Roosevelt's enemies. She was another Great Spirit of moral courage. Like Lincoln, she had within her something that consistently, said "no" to social injustice. Eleanor was able to maintain her moral convictions even as she experienced, herself, the indignities promulgated by FBI's J. Edgar Hoover—whose paranoid spyings about her activities continued until she died. While it is true that Eleanor didn't always do the politically *correct* thing, she constantly implored and pushed her husband, President Franklin D. Roosevelt, and the American public to do the *right* thing.

Both Lincoln and Eleanor Roosevelt were blessed with—or had developed through their experiences in life and with reading books—*the ability to think for themselves.*

Though Eleanor was not financially poor like Lincoln was in his youth, she was poor in a way in which he was rich. She was raised in a family void of emotional acceptance and warmth. Her mother rejected Eleanor, biographers contend, because Eleanor was not beautiful, and beauty was the only requisite for a woman's social success in those days. How, then, can we explain Eleanor's incredible drive, spirit and compassion? Her ability to love?

Perhaps it was her father who gave her just enough love that she survived a horrible situation and grew in toughness and spirit. And, although her father was alcoholic, he did speak of his love for her. It was apparent that he cared for her greatly, but was wasted by his alcoholism and was gone much more often than he was home.

When Eleanor was eight, her mother died. Only two years later, her father also died. Eleanor was sent to live with her grandmother, but although the woman meant well, she had to send Eleanor away to boarding school to protect her from her nearly insane uncles, who were known to have taken shots at neighboring children.

Being sent away to boarding school might have saved Eleanor's life in more than one way. There, for the first time, she made life-long friends. Most importantly for our country, however, she formed her ideas about social justice. Eventually, she would live out those ideas with a blend of wisdom, compassion and common sense.

Even though none of the significant people in Eleanor's life would, in the long run, be loyal to her, she was steadfast in her loyalty to them. The world saw her demonstrate loyalty to our country, time and time again.

Through it all, the difficult childhood and the antagonism of political foes, Eleanor was kind. She never stooped to being less polite or less sensitive to those who maligned her. Neither was she ever heard to malign anyone, nor speak sarcastically about people. I firmly believe she was a respecter of all people, saw them as individuals, and was connected to them, especially the poor and those who were suffering. She must have had a core, a center of beliefs from which she consistently acted.

The High Road. All those present in the United Nations at the time Eleanor was the United States ambassador were amazed and impressed with her response to the Russian ambassador when he criticized her work. In a derisive tone, he asked how he could possibly give any credence to her opinions when she was, after all, only a woman? Eleanor replied in a courteous manner to the ambassador's challenge, asking him to evaluate her, not as a woman, but, instead, by the plausibility of the thoughts she expressed. Ego had never been a problem for Eleanor.

Social Justice and the Search for Truth

Looking back in time, we can see that great leaders like Abraham Lincoln and Eleanor Roosevelt worked as they did for the good of all people. They had an uncommon blend of wisdom, compassion and common sense. Were they, do you suppose, operating out of a special concept of truth?

What Kind of Truth? To the Romans, truth (veritas) was that which could be verified by the senses, i.e., seen, heard and touched. Roman truth had a strong tendency to believe only the hard facts—anything that could be observed and had physical evidence.

Psychologist Wayne Dyer in his book, Wisdom of the Ages, cites examples of great past social injustices using solely Roman truth criteria—facts alone: Joan of Arc was burned at the stake, Herod decreed all first-born males were to be killed, women and African Americans were denied the vote, African Americans were punished for using the same facilities as whites, witches were burned at the stake, Hitler sent millions of Jews to death camps, and so on.

To the Greeks, the truth (aletheia) was different in the sense that it meant that which was *revealed*. Literally, truth meant the "removal of the veil," as in "the veil dropped from his eyes." Truth was something that had a deeper meaning—an inner knowing—a mystery to be intuited and understood, a logos or thought whose words express the meaning of truth at the center of it all.

Psychologist Jean Houston made this interesting statement. "The emphasis may shift to affirming things that are true but not always accurate, rather than just those that are accurate but not true." Which is to say, that effective social justice is neither made up of only intuited/revealed truth nor is it based only on cold hard facts. My own opinion is more in tune with Jean Houston's statement about truth. That is, in order for social justice to take place on a significant level for our society, it must be made up of *both kinds of truth*. As Henry Alford in 1870, quoting the Psalmist said, "'Rivers of water run down mine eyes, because men keep not thy law.'" The Psalmist did not state the facts, but he sent us seeking that which lay within – a truth deeper than fact.

Step by Step. Searching the lives of Abraham Lincoln and Eleanor Roosevelt, one sees within them the ability to drink out of the well from which both "truths" can be drawn. In order to do what they believed to be right, and democratic, as they made each choice along the way, they built within themselves a tower of moral courage.

Wisdom in the Words

Novel Justice. There are certain modern-day novelists who are excellent writers. They write primarily fiction, yet their stories are filled with meaning. Barbara Kingsolver who received an Honorary Doctorate of Letters from her alma mater, DePauw University in Greencastle, Indiana, is one of these writers. Her novel, The Bean Trees, received high acclaim. Kingsolver's women characters learn the value of knowing who lives around them and of building a group into a community. Reading The Bean

Trees can help one experience vicariously how friends, and a group of like-minded people, can be instrumental in improving the quality of life. In some instances, such people, as a group, can help each other survive.

The Shape of Justice and its Internal Geography. Eleanor Roosevelt's power was, as we know, mainly political. She espoused and brought to fruition many good causes. She was also the founder and head of the 1961 Commission of the Status of Women. But Kingsolver, the fiction writer with underlying feminist issues in her novel, evidences a quiet power of her own. Like Eleanor, she is a gentle and kind person, but absolutely sure of herself in the arena of social justice, having explored the internal geography of injustice in her own life.

Robot Girls. Kingsolver shows the injustice and limitations working in the life of young girls. It is as appalling to her as it is to me to see bright, cheerful, alive young girls fall into the trance of cultural expectations—or lack thereof.

Their robot-like behavior, driven by the traditional expectations of parents and society, has resulted in a number of predictable outcomes. Among them, one sees many teenage girls (even middle-school girls) take dangerous chances with their bodies and their futures. Denying the soul of reason and logic, they elevate, and overvalue, all things male—as if their lives depended on having a boyfriend. It is becoming a commonplace experience for girls to experience date rape and physical violence at the hand of "boyfriends." Our culture must help young girls wake-up to their own potential. It is vitally important that girls learn to value being female, and turn away from the negative social programming.

Let's not wait. Let's befriend as many girls in our sphere of influence as we possibly can. Just as important is for all mothers to teach their sons to respect the female. Of course, many girls act out their inner conflicts because they have fathers who either are absent or who do not affirm their daughters for being female. Fathers can be a terrific influence, once they understand the importance of their relationship with their daughters.

41

Kingsolver's lovely flowing prose shows her characters experiencing the hardships of single motherhood. Yet, their woes are interwoven not only with the cares of being single parents but its triumphs as well. With humor and intelligence, she shows us how society and culture understates the capabilities of women, how sexual harassment is destructive to their self-esteem, and how women struggle with childcare issues.

However, as a reader of Kingsolver's novels, I do not feel that she has an axe to grind. She is not "foisting" her social concerns upon the public. Instead, she gently draws the reader into the life experiences of her characters and situations. Two such examples are the priest in the Sanctuary movement—the Underground Railroad started in 1981 to help Central America citizens flee their homes to escape violence and persecution, and the Cherokee Nation during their forced trek to Oklahoma.

The Lottery of a Limited Life. Kingsolver's characters are like plants trying to thrive in the poor soil of social injustice. Yet some, because of strong ties and relationships, flourish like wisteria vines—the "bean trees." As a novelist, Barbara Kingsolver gives equal time to the ugliness of the cultural situation and to the beauty of the world.

Cruel Places Breed Cruel People. Kingsolver speaks for those who cannot speak for themselves. She finds them in small towns across the United States. They are the people without community, those who are so isolated by rejection that their survival is threatened. She stresses the importance of emotional support from others. Cruel places have no sense of community because there is a scarcity of emotional support and no water in the well of hope.

Don't Speak. As a member of what social scientist Gayle Sheehy calls "the silent generation," I understand too well the feeling of not having a voice. My voice is not forthcoming in speaking or debating, but in writing. Consequently, I greatly value any person in our society who, for whatever reason, can give a voice to those who cannot speak.

In Kingsolver's novel, the reader can feel the hope that she wishes to impart. I have heard her say that she *wants* the reader to parlay that hope into power. She *wants* people to know they *can* change the world.

Social justice continues to raise many questions in the American psyche. How can we develop a wider camera angle when we look at social justice? After all, social justice is not a concept whose application is reserved for the few. How can one be true to self and still be responsible to family and community?

Henry David Thoreau struggled with these questions and others in his essay, "Where I Lived and What I Lived For." In his mind, a rigid social existence leads to a life of quiet desperation. And, although they are of different eras, like Kingsolver, Thoreau's hope is for himself and for us—a hope that we elevate our lives by conscious endeavor. (There it is again, that wake-up call.)

A Message in a Dream. Some years ago, I received what I believed to be a kind of wake-up call. I had a dream in which my deceased father appeared, waving his hands as if to get my attention. His expression was kind and expectant. In the dream, he told me, "The early bird gets the worm!" Then he directed my attention across a space as if in time where I saw metal (mental!) file boxes with golden ears of corn suspended in front of them. I have interpreted the dream on several levels. The most pragmatic one is that my father was telling me not to fall asleep, but to wake-up, to stay alert, to gain the life that would then be available to me. To live! He was saying, in a way, not to fall back into the illusion of a life lived by someone else's rules. He was also saying, just as importantly, that thinking for myself would lead to a wonderful "harvest."

"Think About It." I will always be thankful my father encouraged me to think for myself. He did this in another most unusual way. When something puzzled me, I would ask my dad why it had happened, or why the person was behaving in that way. He would often not give an explanation, but simply say, "Now, think about that, Merrily." (Merrily was his nickname for me.) And I would. I would think about it until I had come to my own tentative answer to the question. Sometimes, I would share with him what I thought, and at other times, I would be content with my own thoughts on the matter. I also learned to consider two opposite views when evaluating a situation.

It is important to be able to hold views without letting inconsistencies between our beliefs and our actions disrupt our thinking process. For example, we all know we are going to die. We also know that we must, at the same time, strive to grow and change and make the world a better place—even though we may not be around to see the fruits of our labors.

How Silence Speaks

The Silent Generation. I have mentioned earlier that I am a member of the group of persons whom Gayle Sheehy calls in her book, New Passages, "The Silents." Sheehy was also a member of this Silent Generation, which she has designated as those who were born between 1930-1945. She calls us the "duck and cover" generation.

A bit of history explains the label. The atom bomb was dropped when we were youngsters. As children, we experienced a nation at war—makeshift bomb shelters, air raid drills, blackouts, collecting milkweed pods for filling parachutes, victory gardens, food stamps, gas rationing, and the last years of the Great Depression. We saw our parents give food to "bums" who were starving and afoot. Barns were often used as motels by "travelers." During that time, we children saw but did not understand men who "acted funny." We were told they were shell-shocked, but we didn't know what that meant. Every morning, in school, we proudly faced the flag and said the pledge of allegiance.

One day I overheard an adult talking about a family friend who had been sent home from the war. I wrote a poem that I feel expresses at some level the feeling we had in those days upon seeing these fragmented men of war. Bill DeFoore, a psychologist, poet, and guitarist, set these lines to music. Bill sang and played the poem/song at a meeting of the Fort Worth Poetry Society on September 10, 1992.

"Give Me Your White Roses"

Charlie Tanner came to call
Standing silent by the wall
Where he often came to wait
Taking my bread without a plate.

War had left his mind somewhere
Easier that place to bear
Looked about him for awhile
Then asked of me with pleading smile,

    Please give me your white roses,
    Those atop the backyard gate
    My mother's son has died she says,
    I must take them for she waits.

Waits for roses though he sleeps
Petals tremble, Charlie weeps,
Thinks below in earthen bed
Lays his mother's son who's dead.

I gladly cut the roses faire
Gladly gave the white ones there
Charlie smiled as no other—
For Charlie Tanner had no brother.

    Please give me your white roses
    Those atop the backyard gate
    Mother's son has died she says,
    I must take them for she waits.

What the Silents Learned. Through these early experiences, a great many of the Silents developed certain character traits which continue to be exhibited in their later years. As individuals we learned: 1) Keep your head down and keep working; 2) Work and determination are the price of success (This was my high school class motto.) 3) Keep your own council.

The Silents were strong and, of course...silent. As such they weren't great party people; they were a fairly serious hard-working bunch. It might be supposed that the silent generation would come into their later years angry at having missed so much of their childhood. But not so. It was as if we, with our parents, had been a part of righting a great social injustice.

We also learned optimism for difficult and troubled times. It was as if my generation had a "fix" on what was important versus what was simply to be dealt with and gotten through.

I vividly recall hearing President Franklin Delano Roosevelt say over our floor- model radio, "We have nothing to fear but fear itself." The adults around me echoed this powerful message.

Although the Silents never elected a President of their own, Bill Moyers, Tedd Koppel, Lesley Stahl and Pierre Salinger, were among the role models. Among the women, the Silents were Joan Baez, Janis Joplin, Angela Davis, Gloria Steinem and Oprah Winfry. Later, they would find their voices. Gayle Sheehey found her voice by speaking through her books. A talented researcher, she often gives us gems of information overlooked by others. She has given many others, including myself, a way to look at, to understand, my own childhood in the context of history. Thanks to Gayle Sheehy's research we can also place ourselves more accurately in our culture's system. But it gets even better.

The Good Kids. Sheehy's research reports that The Silent Generation had the lowest incidence of socially aberrant behavior, crime, suicide, illegitimate birth, and teen unemployment. I feel I can personally validate her research, in that not one of my Silent Generation friends was ever jailed, gave birth out of wedlock, or loafed the summer away.

I, myself, grew up on a farm in rural Indiana. Come summer time, my peers and I worked in the cornfields. There was a man in Wabash County, Chester Troyer, who held the title of "Corn King of the World." My little group of girls, in order to make money for college, or to fulfill various other dreams, worked out-of-doors in the summer months for Mr. Troyer. We cross-pollinated seed corn, de-tasseled and hoed corn eight hours a day. Blisters, callouses and sunburn abounded! To this day, when I see day laborers or migrant workers in the fields, I know their experience. The Silents learned to work, and to do any work they could put their hands to.

A Stalled Life. After the war was over, women left their important war time jobs and went back into housework and raising kids—the job society said they must do, even though their role wasn't recognized as important. They became the undervalued part of the population, too far out of the loop for influence or power.

A Sensitive Social Conscience. However, the Silent women went back to school in mass after age 40. Gloria Steinem formed the National Political Caucus, and we silent women were on the way to developing a highly sensitive social conscience. Many of us read Betty Freidan's book the Feminine Mystique with much interest.

Silents—*men and women*—have turned out to be good at mediating and counseling. They appear able to reach out to people of all ages and races, as if they know there is a common thread that binds all people. As President Clinton pointed out in his State of the Union Address in early 2000, "geneticists say all human beings' DNA is 99.9% the same."

Adopting Jerry. Although my friend Jerry may not fit, exactly, into the profile of a Silent—he may be a "tad" older—I think he, and people like him, should be included in our group. Here's why. In December of 1999, we received a Christmas letter from Jerry and his wife Rosemary. Jerry and I grew up on the same block in Wabash, Indiana. Our fathers were friends who had great coon dogs, and the men, often accompanied by their sons, would race through the brambles and the bushes, wading creeks and ponds on cold moonlight nights to follow the baying dogs.

Later in his life, Jerry, became a PhD marine biologist, preferring to hunt the warmer waters of the coral reefs, and President (now retired) of Western Washington University, in Everson, Washington.

But, with all of these accomplishments, the only photograph Jerry has of himself as a child is in a picture of my father with his coon dogs. In the photograph, little Jerry is sitting on the garage steps looking toward my father with eyes full of admiration. He says my dad was his hero, an inspiration for his own life's work, and a model of courage.

I want to share with you Jerry's poignant letter—to share the words of a great man of science who struggles with a highly sensitive social conscience. When I wrote asking for permission to reprint his letter in this book, he responded with his typically generous reply: "Please feel free to use any portion of my Christmas letter for anything you wish. It is an extract from my field journal."

Reading the letter, one feels he would give anything to change the backward culture about which he writes and help the people, especially the children trapped within that culture.

The Letter

First of all we are alive. Secondly we are pleased to be so. We spent 1997 and 1998 plus a wee bit of 1999 on an atoll called Abaiang in the central Pacific. Our intent was to do good. It is difficult to explain what we did, whether good or bad, so I am sending the following sample from my field journal to give a realistic though not merry, taste of our experience.

FROM ABAIANG FIELD JOURNAL
October 29, November 1, 1997
October 29, 1997; Wednesday (Ocean)~1343-1600 hrs.
A Cacophony of Sensations

Some days ago, I poured a mixture of water and half cement, half foram beach sand down the burrow of a coconut crab, *Birgus latro*, near the beach behind our house. I wanted to see what the home of this remarkable land crab looked like. There was Portland Cement left over from construction of the new science building and I took a bit for this purpose.

I started trying to unearth the casting using a rusty old table spoon someone had long since abandoned on the beach and quickly realized this tool was no match for the tough roots, the cobble and the sand which kept collapsing back into the hole. I went to the school custodian and borrowed a shovel.

In half an hour, the casting was free and rested on our bwia as I refilled the large hole. The outline of the crab's home was now known to me.

At about 1530 hours, the tide was high and I walked to the sandy shore behind our thatched house in search of good ghost crab holes fit for casting. I continued past some folks bobbing about in the waves just off shore in the meter deep water and waved at them as my nose detected the strong, sweetish odor of human feces along the beach. Not sure that going for a dip here is wise when a full complement of students is in attendance. Please understand, the beach is the toilet.

I walked with my eyes locked on the drift lines and as always, was amazed at the variety of interesting items cast ashore by the waves. Items in the drift are indicators of the character of the living reef. I passed Auaiang (the boy's residential area) and continued for about 100 m beyond. On the return, I walked through Auaiang and saw many boys assembled in the large, metal roofed maneaba (meeting place). Intermittently, I heard gales of laughter.

Curious, I drew closer, heard the thump of a stout stick and saw it land on legs and buttocks. One after another, boys passed before the teacher who was a former policeman, reformed alcoholic and now the man in charge of Tabwiroa (the school) boys. His task now was to beat young male students for some infraction. With a 5-cm thick club, WHANG! WHANG! BAM! This 2 meter tall, enormously strong man struck each child four or five times. He hit them solidly and energetically. How many boys were disciplined this day and for what I did not know but none cried, none shouted, all hurt and held themselves as they left the maneaba. The audience laughed as each blow fell, I did not.

As I walked across the playing field, I heard moaning in the distance. I assumed it was one of the beaten children or maybe a dog being butchered for food.

I encountered an imatang (foreign) friend who has been in Kiribati for many years about to go fishing, which he did at every opportunity just as I go to the reef as often as possible. I think the poor guy has developed a dislike for every body. Sometimes I think I have too. I reached the house as another imatamg walked by and I could see that she had lost weight and seems ill though she is very brave.

49

At 1600 hours I walked into the kitchen and found Rosemary working furiously on her laptop computer preparing for next day's classes. Tough lady, hard worker.

The whole scene here is surrealistic, almost macabre, certainly very strange.

As I said, today was a cacophony of sensations.

November 1, 1997; Saturday (Ocean)

At 1000 hours, Rosemary and I turned left from the Entry and walked along the drift lines and in a desultory fashion looked for items of interest. Our hearts are heavy. The moaning I had heard day before yesterday was neither a beaten child nor a dog. It was one of our finest students, a young man named Teatata who excelled in science in Form 4 Blue (author's explanation: this is the name of a specific class in their school). He suffered from Hepatitis B. He died this morning. A good boy, in the top 3 of my science students, tragic. I weep. It is easy to hate this place. This bright young man was in Rosemary's home form, Form 4 Blue, and in my science class. I was especially upset because he seems to have died of hepatitis, a raging viral epidemic in this place. Two forms, A and B (perhaps C too), seem to be most common with A infecting the greater number of students. Hepatitis B is, of course, more severe than A and it is probably the one that killed Teatata. At least eleven students in Form 4 Blue have had one or the other this year. Much Hepatitis A can be blamed on what I call "the Hepatitis Factory."

The Hepatitis Factory is a large 1 m diameter, aluminum pot filled with rainwater and sugar. Students drink from the pot using only a few plastic cups which are often thrown back into the pot after use. An unwashed hand reaches into the tub and seizes a community cup, the owner of the hand gulps the sweet water, throws the cup back into the tub and it is seized by another unwashed hand. Please understand, the hand owner has at least once that day gone to the beach, squatted and defecated, cleansed his/her anal area with a folded coconut frond leaflet, without washing hands. Washing hands is not easy here. The Hepatitis A virus is spread not only by fecal waste but also by saliva and flies.

Of course saliva easily passes to the cups. If one wanted to spread Hepatitis A, it would be hard to develop a method more efficient than the "Hepatitis Factory."

Hepatitis B is a different story. It behaves much like the retrovirus, which causes AIDS; i.e. it is not spread by casual contact. The virus must be introduced directly into the blood vascular system, which could happen by tattooing with unclean needles or anal sex. But, tattooing is common and use of unsterile needles 100%.

Hepatitis A could be reduced by simple and obvious changes in the way liquid refreshments are handled. Hepatitis B could be reduced by eliminating tattooing.

Now I knew all this before Teatata died, but I never raised hell with the right people. I complained to fellow imatangs (foreigners) and spoke to my classes but did not make issue at staff meetings, with the principal, the sisters, the brothers i.e., the people who ran the place. Had I done so, the Factory might have been closed or cleaned up months ago and perhaps the tattooing could have been stopped and perhaps...? Whatever, I walked the drift line today with deep feelings of sorrow mixed with guilt.

We walked on the sand to Porites Rock then out to the crest, then along the crest to a point straight out from the Island Hospital pigpen. Then at mid-flat we went back to Nei Mama (where two Tabwiroa boys were killed in 1995) and on to the crest at Big Trap. We were back at the house by 1230 hours.

OBSERVATIONS: At 1036 hours near the crest off Porites Rock, we watched an 8 cm long sea hare which had an internal shell (*Aplysia*) inch swiftly along the bottom in 5 cm of water. In the same area we watched vast number of brittle stars.

ENOUGH—Jerry and Rosemary 12/18/99

*****

Post Script: In a report on Monday, February 21, 2000, in The Fort Worth Star-Telegram, 58 historians of various political persuasions answered a survey by C-Span, the cable TV network, to rank the U.S. presidents. On President's Day, the results were in. Abraham Lincoln was first in light of his, "crises leadership, administrative skills, vision, pursuit of justice and 'performance within the context of the times.'" He was followed by Franklin

Delano Roosevelt, George Washington, Theodore Roosevelt and Harry S. Truman, of the nation's 41 chief executives.

Of more recent presidents, George Bush ranked 20th; Jimmy Carter, 22nd; Gerald Ford, 23rd; and Nixon 25th, more toward the middle. The lowest-ranked presidents were William Henry Harrison, Warren G. Harding, Franklin Pierce, Andrew Johnson and, last, James Buchanan. Clinton, who was rated 21st overall, was rated last in moral authority, one rung below former President Nixon.

From the rankings above it is apparent that there are certain elements we must look for in candidates for elective office. Character is the most essential element, especially where it is supported by vision, and courage.

Chapter 2 References

Dyer, Wayne W., Wisdom of the Ages, HarperCollins Publisher, NY, NY, 1998.

Benet', Stephen Vincent, John Brown's Body, The Heritage Press, NY, NY, 1927.

Benet', Stephen Vincent, Western Star, Farrar and Rinehart, NY, NY, 1943.

Lincoln, Abraham, The Poems of Abraham Lincoln, Applewood Books, Bedford, Massachusetts, 1991

Friedan, Betty, The Feminine Mystique, W.W. Norton, N.Y., N.Y., 1963.

Gray, Paul, "The Millennium," Time magazine, NY, NY, December 31, 1999.

Houston, Jean, PhD, A Mythic Life, HarperCollins, NY, NY, 1996.

Sheehey,Gayle, Character, America's Search for Leadership, Morrow, NY, NY, 1988.

Sheehy, Gail, New passages, Random House, NY, NY, 1995.

Naisbitt, John and Patricia Aburdene, Megatrends 2000, Avon Books. NY, NY, 1999.

Kingsolver, Barbara, The Bean Tree, HarperCollins, NY, NY, 1988.

Peck, M. Scott, M.D., <u>Further Down the Road Less Traveled</u>, Simon & Schuster, NY, NY, 1993.

Thoreau, David Henry, "Where I Lived, and What I Lived For," in Masters of American Literature, Ed., Johnson, Paul and Simpson, The Riverside Press, Cambridge Massachusetts, 1959.

Lincoln, Abraham, <u>The Poems of Abraham Lincoln</u>, Applewood Books, Distributed by The Globe Pequot Press, Bedford, Massachusetts, 1991.

CHAPTER 3: SERPENTS vs. THE DOVES

All religious sects are different because they come from men; morality is everywhere the same because it comes from God.—Voltaire

It is not spiritual people who are sick, but the "religious" where beliefs are neurotic and rigid.—Carl Jung

You may have noticed it is becoming more and more common for rugged football players in post game interviews to shout praise and thanks to God for the victory.

There is a religious revival afoot, and "football witnessing" is only the tip of the iceberg. But who, may I ask, is getting "revived" in the battle of religion vs. religion? Will there be a winner in the "Super Bowl" of the "Holiest?" Whatever the answer, it's in the air and everywhere..."the times they are achangin."

I think it fair to say at the outset that the quote from Voltaire reflects what scholars, religious and secular, have found when comparing all the great religions of the world. Essentially, most of them are based on a foundation very much like the Ten Commandments.

Having said that, let's take another look at the religious revival. A quarter of a century ago, no one saw it coming. Most of the experts in the United States thought religion was "dead in the water," and that the great white shark of modern technology was circling in for the kill. As the 20th century dawned, intellectuals George Bernard Shaw and H. G. Wells both thought religion was on its way out.

A Many-Sided Revival. Ninety years after Shaw and Wells' predictions, a pervasive religious wave is sweeping our country. Naisbitt and Aburdene predicted this in their social research work on megatrends. But this revival is "pantheistic" in the sense that it is being experienced across all religious fronts and is multi-denominational.

The large scale religious mergers that were predicted are happening. More than nine Christian denominations voted to move toward a broad affiliation of churches. Can other mergers be far behind? For this merging to happen, some very longstanding differences have apparently been overcome. I have heard the opinion expressed on more than one occasion that Roman Catholic Priests, at some time in the near future, will be free to marry. Theologically speaking, it seems as if the face of God could even change color and sex—but will those things change back again a millennium later? A woman as Greek or Roman Patriarch? A woman as President? Just asking. "The times they are achangin.'"

Somebody Do Something!

According to The Harris Poll Election 2000—The State of the Nation, great numbers of Americans feel our country is living in a moral cesspool and also know that religion is a shaper of behavior. Still, one does not have to be a believer to be worried about morals and values. The Poll shows that 88% of the people who claim the title Christian see morals and values in poor-to-fair shape. Sharing this view are 69% of Catholics, 70% of Agnostics and 80% of Atheists.

Patricia Aburdene in her book about megatrends in 2010 says expect "a big trend for value-driven managers as opposed to the star CEOs; and many will expand their spiritual practice into their working lives. More people will invest responsibly and change the course of even the largest companies."

Baby boomers (those born in the years immediately following World War II) have taken the lead in the religious revival. Some are going back to mainline churches and taking their kids to Sunday school; others are off to explore the humanistic New Age movements and Eastern religions. Meanwhile, the evangelicals and the fundamentalists are doing what they have always done best—seeking additional membership—and using high tech options and TV to draw in the new members.

High-Tech Soul Saving. A Jesuit publication, America, describes fundamentalism as, "a reactionary emotional movement that develops within cultures experiencing social crises." (That "social crises" phrase surely does have a familiar ring to it, doesn't it? In spite of it all, I do confess I like Billy Graham. There is something about him that has the air of authenticity.)

Fundamentalism relieves people of having to think through religious questions for themselves. The decisions and any answers are made for them. In times of great social change, most cultures seek to escape to a way that promises them solutions to their problems and answers to their questions. For some individuals, this works quite well. For others, it does not work at all.

Preachers who use the technology of television and cable channels to bring in income and save souls are on the cutting edge when it comes to gaining adherents. Jimmy Swaggart, a television evangelist before his awkward departure, broadcast in 140 countries and in fifteen different languages. Jim and Tammy Baker spoke to over twelve million households and Jerry Falwell's 1987 television evangelism netted him $91 million. Although television evangelists' followers and profits are declining, non-the-less, they have demonstrated considerable talent for blending preaching and the technology of television.

Gospel Gin. Father Leo Booth, an Episcopal priest, made an interesting discovery about alcohol addiction and religious abuses. Although he felt many people would react to his ideas with anger and confusion, he wrote about his discovery in his book, Breaking the Chains. The book is an enlightened look at the roots of religious addiction. If you prepare to read it, be ready for a direct, compassionate book written without pretense.

Father Booth shows us who, how and why certain individuals are at risk of joining a cult...or becoming addicted to a television evangelist. One can see after reading his words how young people get involved with cults and gangs—they are looking for an escape from the pain and loneliness of adolescence. His statistics show us that teens are more vulnerable to the appeal of cults while older, lonely people use television evangelism for a "fix."

A 12-Step program is helpful for the religious addict. What is surprising is how similar are the backgrounds of both alcoholics and fundamentalists. It is not uncommon for a recovering alcoholic to confess, "I was seeking God in a bottle." A fundamentalist says, "God told me that.... It must have come from God."

The 12-Step program for alcoholics works well with religious addicts because, as with alcoholics, each step calls the addicted person back to reality and away from an escape into denial and illusions. The safety of group support is also considered an important feature for the addict's recovery.

Father Booth was also instrumental in organizing "Fundamentalists Anonymous" meetings—a program that teaches the message that the miracle they seek is within themselves rather than in a magical, dysfunctional solution.

Of course, any compulsive or obsessive trait shows itself as a lack of balance. The "out of balance" psychological defenses used by the religious addict are the same as those employed by the alcoholic. Booth lists these traits as: rationalizing, justifying, projecting, blaming, judging, intellectualizing, analyzing, explaining, theorizing, generalizing, quibbling, debating (arguing), sparring, questioning another's integrity, switching, and acting smug (superior). God becomes the "drug of choice," a "gospel gin," that soothes all pain. Psychologist Jean Houston agrees with Booth in that she says, "The double threat of alcohol and Christian fundamentalism lays waste to our lives."

The Antagonist

A Badly Twisted Spiritual Serpent. This section on antagonists could be used as a follow-up to Kenneth Hauck's book, Antagonists in the Church. I say this because the antagonistic personality may be one reason why more and more people—despite the powerful combination of old time religion and new technology—are saying *no* to religion and *yes* to spirituality. A twisted outlook marks the antagonistic person, as he or she elevates into the perceived realm of power.

I dedicate this chapter to anyone who has been attacked by an antagonist and to those who have become hurt or discouraged with the pain caused by an antagonistic attack—in the church *or in any other place*. It is time to raise our consciousness and learn to deal with these destructive people.

I feel compelled to write about the problem of antagonism in our society because I have witnessed first-hand the suffering caused by antagonistic people. The effects on a person's or group's life are malevolent. If we, as a culture, are to move forward, these attacks *must* stop. Through knowledge, we can certainly lower the number of fatalities. This goal *can* be obtained if we "dove types" get a handle on how to deal with antagonists.

Kenneth C. Haugh, a pastor and clinical psychologist, defines antagonists as "individuals who, on the basis of nonsubstantive evidence, go out of their way to make insatiable demands, usually attacking a person or performance of others. These attacks are selfish in nature, tearing down rather than building up, and are frequently directed toward those in a leadership capacity." Haugh has experienced first-hand the attacks of an antagonist . He stated that this experience was so personally devastating, it nearly ended his career.

Let me say before going any further, that the antagonistic personality can show up at any time and at any place in your life. Rest assured, unless you live under a rock, at some point you will find this character in your viewfinder. It is not a matter of "if" you will dance with an antagonist, but when...because they are everywhere, woven into the fabric of our society.

Although Hauck's book is about the antagonist in the church, one could easily substitute the word church with hospital, neighborhood, club, association, business, institution, school, or home. The first thing to remember about the destructive personality type is that they are attracted to service-oriented, small, warm groups of giving people. They almost always rise to the higher rungs within an organization.

Most members in these kinds of small, service groups have gathered to perform some kind of work or service, or to help society in some way. The antagonistic person is immediately drawn to this kind of group, and begins to "infiltrate." Their goal is to get control of the group. They are driven by power. They must have power even if it destroys and/or divides the group.

MARILYN GILBERT KOMECHAK, PhD

The Friendly Others

Before the antagonist joins the group, the membership is accepting, open, friendly, available and *unaware*—the *friendly others*, as I call them. They naively assume everyone has the best interests of the group at heart. They are unaware that there are people who, because of their neurosis, are basically destructive to a group.

I emphasize the word *unaware* because so often the friendly others see themselves, and subsequently everyone else, as if they all have the same agenda—the same goals. They assume most people have the same motivations as they—to do good—to get along.

The anger that underlies the antagonist's veneer of good cheer, that of the good ol' boy or girl, eventually will be seen, but often it is too late. The antagonist seems to have a radar beacon which picks up on any power voids and allows him to begin maneuvering to fill those voids. Unfortunately, the friendly others, the naive ones, let the aggressive behavior go rather than challenge it. After all, nice folks don't cause disturbances—or should they?

After the antagonist gets into a position of power or influence, he (or she) will proceed to become the center of attention. The antagonist, eager to exert power, will almost always do so in a heavy-handed manner. Ultimately, he will become a "mini-Hitler."

By various manipulations which will be discussed later, he targets the person who is the group leader in order to usurp the power base. Hauck says it should come as no surprise that he targets the member who has the most leadership. The antagonist shows his true colors by acting out with disruptive behavior or irrational attacks on others. This is so often, at least at first, a subtle thing, but it will be cleverly played out.

Collecting "Brown Stamps"

Hauck says, "Angry at self, the world, and any convenient situation or person, antagonists seem to wander through life seeking, inviting, and collecting injustices against themselves…Their life style is more like that of a heat seeking missile. They track their prey with deadly accuracy." In my mind's eye, I visualize these people wearing combat boots and brandishing swords. Yet, they can also play "poor me" with a vengeance.

In past years, some of my clients, my friends and several close family members have been the subject of attacks. I have witnessed many accounts of an antagonist's attack to break (or nearly so) the spirits of these people. Two of these persons were active church members, each one of a different denomination. A third person was an employee of a large company, a fourth person, a skilled land developer, two were schoolteachers, and one worked as a university administrator. But attacks can occur in any professional or social group.

How Do They Get Control? The process is fairly standard. At first, the antagonist will build up the leader's ego, particularly if the leader is respected by the group or has been designated to be leader. The antagonist will criticize the person who did the job before, and tell the leader how *he* is so much better. At first, the antagonist is chummy and charming and fun to be with. The leader finds himself basking in the compliments. Hauck warns to watch out for the red "Buddy Flag."

Antagonists have an air of superiority that will later become quite evident, especially when they begin to come to the leader in "confidence," to "share" a criticism, saying that "everybody else feels the same way." Yet, if the leader tries to find out who "all the others are," the antagonist will say he can't, in good conscience, reveal what he's been told in secret.

Next comes the situation where he argues openly with the leader before the group and tries to prove him wrong. If the leader has any kind of "weakness," he will find it and use that information in such as way as to unnerve, or humiliate, all the while acting as if what he is doing is for the leader's own good. It is reasonable for the leader to feel as if he is being unfairly punished! This technique is commonly known as "stabbing in the back."

In every case I am familiar with, this has been the process. Criticisms grow until the victim's career itself is jeopardized, or the person is so miserable in the situation that he changes careers or positions in order to leave the situation. Of course, that is exactly what the antagonist is hoping will happen—that the leader will leave and he can take over the post of authority.

Conflict Can Help If It's Healthy. Another sign of dealing with an antagonist is that the kind of trouble stirred up is more than the typical disagreement. Don't misunderstand. Conflict, as you know, is a part of life and is experienced in all societies. Resolving a *healthy* conflict improves the quality of life, and strengthens a group's base values. Unfortunately, too many good-natured people try to avoid conflict, often at any cost.

A Flex Defense

Survival Strategies If Attacked. Hauck lists his attack strategies as: 1) Don't let 'em see you sweat, 2) Never talk with them on a one-to-one basis. (Be sure there are other people present.), 3) Gather your forces around you (other supportive people) and present a unified front they can't penetrate, 4) Meet them on your own turf, at your convenience and (Hauck suggests), for no more than one hour, 5) Be as noncommittal as possible, 6) Do behave confidently, and 7) Proceed with your job or task in the best manner you can muster. (Remember Eleanor Roosevelt who never lost her dignity even in the face of great efforts to dislodge her from her post?)

Don't Become Antagonistic Yourself. A BIG WORD OF WARNING. Examine *yourself* for any signs of antagonism. Falling into the same trap will complicate your life in an unbelievable way. In the long run, an overly aggressive life style will not work for you. While each of us acts antagonistically at times, a few hostile words or acts do not an antagonist make. Still, watch yourself; let go of the need to retaliate. Focus instead on what you can do or say; prime among those things is getting needed rest and relaxation. In other words, take care of yourself. Paying attention to your own needs is difficult, especially in a high stress time, but it will help greatly in the long run.

<u>Courtside</u>. It is not often that the battle between antagonist and victim is taken into the courts; however, it does happen. It is my perception that the courts are more and more frequently being asked to intervene.

Dr. Ben Strickland, a life style consultant to businesses and institutions, says there are at least three strategies for dealing with an aggressive person: 1) If an antagonist bores in on you in a meeting, acknowledge what they are saying but then, "pass the hot potato." For example, "I hear you, Betty…John what are your thoughts on this?" 2) Refuse to shoot it out with them at the waterhole; they are at their best when fighting and they will *never* quit arguing. They do *not* respond well to being reasoned with. 3) Do them some small unexpected kindness. Strickland says, and rightly so, that kindness throws them off. They do not know how to respond to those kinds of gestures. For example, when you both arrive at the coke machine at the same time, say, "Let me get this."

Hauck wisely suggests not to tell the antagonist he needs counseling because this will infuriate him. He also states that the person who is attacked should forgive the person who has done the damage. It is known that when we are unforgiving, and hold on to a grudge, we are at risk for developing depression. Our depression will have negative effects on our friends, family and employers, and could eventuate in health problems. In effect, we are giving all our power to our attacker. However, *this forgiveness must not be blind*!

Here is a case where "forgive and forget," should not be paired together. Forgive, yes, but do not forget. Psychologists know that antagonists have an *insatiable* craving for "war." Like ancient warlords, their entire lives, actions, and egos are dedicated to "knocking off" their opponents. Antagonists crave conflict. They must have it. It is like oxygen to their existence. So you must be wary, forgiving, *but not forgetting*, as you will need to watch for further eruptions.

<u>What Are You Sensing</u>? Do not place all your faith in the techniques listed here because it is also of utmost importance to acknowledge your own feelings. This allows you to act in a more congruent manner. Pay attention to your own intuition, and you will know when you are being set-up, manipulated and/or bullied.

You will gain more insight this way and become more comfortable in using the strategies Hauck suggests.

As an example, let's say you will be running a scheduled meeting. By being aware in advance of the possibility of antagonistic behavior, you can inform one or two of the group members of this possibility. They can be asked to intervene when antagonistic behavior begins by saying something like "Let's get on with the work we came to do. Let's get back to the agenda."

A Few Good Moves. Antagonists favor the "divide and conquer" principle. They are good at setting up triangulation. That is, a third party (guess who) gets two leaders or group members to fight between themselves. This power-grabbing ploy has worked since the beginning of time. As Edwin Burke, English statesman warned, "All it takes for the forces of destruction to win is for good people to do nothing."

Serpents 1, The Doves 3. People ask me, "Why are there antagonists?" Antagonism results when the "spiritual space" within the person is void; we know today that our society has large pockets of spiritual scarcity.

Although there are answers to be found, and different levels of analysis, a lecture given by psychiatrist, M. Scott Peck analyzed the course of religious development in life. His work sprang from that analysis and is connected to James Fowler's Stages of Faith, a book that is required reading for most seminarians.

Peck is the first to admit that he is careful about using the word, "religious," preferring the word spiritual or spirituality in regard to matters of a religious nature. This is because, he says, so much damage has been done to people in the name of religion.

In Peck's book, Further down the Road Less Traveled, he summarizes the ideas he was presenting some years ago in his lecture at the University Christian Church in Fort Worth, Texas. I will try to reiterate them here as I remember them.

Peck's theory finds most folks falling into one of four categories or stages of religious/spiritual development. Keep in mind that these are not rigid categories. Any one individual may circle back through these stages at any time in life. Peck sees each stage as more or less a way station on the journey toward spiritual growth.

The categories are from least developed to highly developed: 1) The serpents (or amoral people) 2) The professional religious and church laymen and laywomen 3) The doubters or agnostics, and 4) The truly spiritual people. (These are the people who have a direct pipeline to God or a higher power.)

This four-step concept of religious/spiritual development is not as rigid as it first appears. Peck says we all apparently move in and out of these stages throughout our lives. We may move through these consecutive stages from one to four or we may become stuck in one stage for a lifetime. I believe the people who get stuck most frequently are those individuals for whom change (or accepting change), of any kind, is most difficult.

Remember Your Adolescence? We can parallel spiritual development with human psychological development. Adolescence is a well-known stage, and fortunately, most of us move past that. However, you may have seen others, or perhaps even yourself, regress to an earlier stage in your life. A 40-year-old who begins acting like a teen again is one example. In our spiritual development we can also regress, become childishly unrealistic. But then we can also move forward. To evolve spiritually, to lead a meaningful life, we must not take any of the tempting shortcuts such as becoming addicted to religion, a person, a bottle, sex, power, or food.

The Pulley System. Peck also asks that we keep in mind that most people are where they need to be in terms of their own, personal, religious development. He suggests that we accept other people and ourselves *where we are* and help each other, as we can.

In his lecture he spoke of the pulley system of helping: Of the four categories or stages of religious/spiritual development, the "twos" are those who can best help the "ones", the "threes" can help the "twos", and the "fours" can help the "threes". Each group pulls the other group up. However, the "fours" and the "ones" are too far apart in their development to be effective with each other.

<u>Who's on First</u>? I want to take a minute here to describe the amoral "serpent" personality, as it is the most dangerous to society. An amoral person is one who is frequently found in the ward of a mental hospital or on the front page of the newspaper. Although this person may be an alcoholic, a murderer, or insane, he may function at a high level and hold a position in government or business. Lying is a way of life for this type of person.

<u>People of the Lie</u>. This is the label that Peck gives to the "ones." In fact, he has written a book by the same title. Some amorals can discipline themselves enough to gain high standing in society. Think of the ministers of large congregations who have been jailed and of those politicians who have risen to the highest levels of our government. Lives based on lies.

<u>Who's in Church</u>? When I walk into a church or a worship service, I suspect that in the pews around me are people of differing spiritual development—ranging all the way from one to four. The minister or priest may be at any one of the stages of spiritual development! If the congregation is largely made up of "twos" and the minister is a "four," the "twos" will usually run him or her off. They do not trust the openness or the spirituality of the person who can follow the *spirit* of the Word, but whose life does not adhere to the rules or to dogma.

And, sad to say, very few "threes," the doubters or agnostics, will be found in church. The questions presented by the "twos" will cause the "threes" to leave because the doubters do not like to be challenged. It is too hard for them to tolerate. Questions shake their tightly built religious structure. The "twos" also find it hard to welcome the "threes" on a continuing basis.

The "ones" will usually develop a cult-like following and may suck the church dry financially. Although they at first move cautiously, they can use charm, power and lies to manipulate the church members and gain power and money.

<u>Hollywood Knows</u>. A movie was made some years ago, "Mrs. Sulfol," starring Diane Keeton. She plays the part of a warden's wife. It is her job to pass out Bibles to the prisoners. During this activity she talks to individual prisoners about the Bible's message.

However, as sometimes happens to "twos" trying to save "ones," she came under the spell of a charming prisoner and was pulled back into the mire of the "ones". Finally, we see her aid him in aking a jailbreak. As they make their break for freedom, prison guards riddle their get-away car with bullets, killing them both.

Occasionally, I read in the newspaper about a lawyer (this person may be male or female) who has defended a person charged as a criminal. In a few instances the lawyer has clandestinely joined the criminal in the amoral activity, or even married the criminal. I would imagine that within those kinds of marriages, "playing cops and robbers," remains a way of life.

Nobody Knows the Trouble I've Seen. The "twos" helping "ones" is dangerous. As you may recall, the "ones" are not capable of feeling empathy. The task of soulsaving is fraught with risk. Not only are the "twos" jeopardizing their own safety, but they also run the risk of ones exerting strong pressure the other way. As with "Mrs. Solful," the two can be drawn back into the one's amoral lifestyle. In fundamentalist churches this is called "backsliding," definitely a lower stage of religious development.

Who Would Have Thought? As I said elsewhere, literature can be a great means for helping people change or evolve. It is almost as if we become what we are through reading. I know in my own life, and in the lives of many of my friends, books have been the "change agent."

I can vividly recall reading, Girl of the Limberlost at age ten. In hindsight, I see that Gene Stratton Porter's book opened a way for me to become my own person. It was as if the author was giving me permission to find my own path and passion in life. I could overcome obstacles and troubles and be who I wanted to be. Ultimately this "me" would be accepted by others. My mother gave me the book. I doubt that she realized, at least at the time, that she was handing me a way out of the strictures under which she herself had lived as a girl.

The following poem illustrates the power of literature to change lives, and at the same time says, "when the pupil is ready, the teacher will come." The poem is true in its essence.

Hubbard Sings Rilke

He stole his grandmama's Pontiac, smoked cocaine
With Lorraine until his mind went slack—after he was
baptized by a Bible salesman—yet, ol' Ray Wiley, he's still
alive.
Must mean white-trash angels *do* exit…insists the record
salesman.

Though everybody knew he was one *loco gringo*,
He played guitar, sang other people's songs, drunk or
drugged.
All year long Ray Wiley kept giggin; on and on
But you never saw any of his music in the record stores.

One day, with nothing else to do, he opened up a book
Letters from one poet to another, read them all in solitude
As if they were addressed to him, until he found a map that
took him to the heart of meaning—wrote songs and read
some nights 'til 3.

Ray Wiley transfused himself with each letter's blood-wind
words,
Letters so salvific he rode them out like a Restless Knight,
To crusade up slopes of old perceptions, challenge the
devil, a hypocrite,
A femme fatale in river beds dried-up with desolation.

The record man ponders as he's ringing up the sale,
speaking like a backwoods preacher after Saturday night's
revival…
Did Ray Wiley turn because he was drawn to a halo of
light?
Or because his hide was roasting in the heat?

But had the record salesman really listened to the *new* Ray
Wiley play,
The chances are…he would have heard a poet singing.

(A 19-year-old Ray Wiley Hubbard wrote the Texas-hippie anthem, "Up Against the Wall You Red-necked Mother," a song made famous by Jerry Jeff Walker. Hubbard went "hitless" for the next 30 years until his new 1999 CD hit, "Crusades of a Restless Knight". Letters to A Young Poet, written by poet Rainer Maria Rilke between 1903 and 1908, was the book that inspired Hubbard.)

(After liner notes by Geoffrey Himes and John T. Davis, Austin, Texas.)

Generic Christian

The Generic Christian? "What does that mean," I asked myself when I first read those words on a bumper sticker. One does not usually see "generic" and Christian together since generic means, at least in pharmaceuticals, not protected by trademark.

However, it wasn't hard to make the leap to understanding, to "get," the meaning of the words on the bumper sticker. My perception is that a generic Christian is one who lives life like a "Brand Name" Christian does, only without all the division, dogma, politics, advertising and amoral destructive infighting.

A generic Christian would probably fit nicely into Peck's groups of "threes" and "fours". These are people who simultaneously do what is good for themselves as well as others. They see to it that good things happen and that destruction is avoided, if at all possible.

Ruminating about generic Christians causes me to think of this analogy. In my imagination, I see "Brand Name" Christians like the Separatists (The Pilgrims) standing, stymied, on the dock. They wanted to board the Mayflower for the New World, but there were too few to come up with the money to pay for their passage. Their hopes were dashed unless they could convince others to make the journey with them. Only then might they be able to sail onward and fulfill their destiny.

The men went out and scoured the town until they found enough others who would pay their own fare and board with them.

In the ship's log these additional people, who were not a part of the original separatist group, were referred to as "Strangers." However, it was those strangers, among them John Alden and Miles Standish, who were most instrumental in helping the Pilgrims survive the crossing and the landings at Provincetown and Plymouth and possessed the skills, compassion and intelligence to help The Separatists survive.

History reports that the "Strangers" did not participate in the rituals and prayers of the Pilgrims, but that they stood respectfully apart. However, some of the Mayflower children married "Strangers," and of these people, both women and men, there were some that went on to eventually fight in the Revolutionary War.

Generic Christians, that is, all spiritual people, may be the force keeping organized religion alive. It may be that these generic spirits are responsible for supporting and encouraging the religious revival we are experiencing today. It is something to think about.

The Link. Many religious teachers, leaders and heads of monasteries and convents have come to realize a profound truth: Without emotional development, a person's spiritual development cannot take place. (Notice it does not say without intellectual development, spiritual development cannot take place.) Consequently, many priests and nuns have been referred to me over the years. It has been a genuine pleasure to know them. Although I am a member of a different religious persuasion, we were able to do some good work in therapy.

When German philosopher Friedrich Nietzche made his stunning pronouncement in 1882 that, "God is dead," he was speaking for intellectuals who put their belief in what could be proven by facts, by science. Thus, they assumed religious faith would die, too.

But, as I have noted earlier, the incredible has happened. In the beginning of the 21st Century, a religious revival is sweeping the country. Yet, I'm wondering if our current religious revival will mean an increase in emotional and spiritual development as well. Only with spiritual development will the current revival survive and have a permanent impact.

What's Prayer Got to Do With it? Of late, however, there have been some encouraging signs. We are seeing something truly amazing—medical research has found a link between science and prayer. The implication of that research is that science and spirituality, used together, can be a significant force to promote and bring about healing.

A study published in the Southern Medical Journal in 1988, pointed the way to this conjunction of science and spirituality. In a San Francisco hospital, it was found that of the 201 coronary patients who had no one praying for them were twice as likely to suffer congestive heart failure as those patients for whom strangers prayed. Also, those patients were four times more likely to have a heart attack.

Herbert Benson, president of Harvard's Mind/Body Medical Institute has studied the effects of combining medicine and prayer. As a result, he strongly advocates integrating behavioral and relaxation therapies in the healing process, along with meditation.

Journalist Michael McManus wrote about a study of 91,000 people in rural Maryland who were weekly church attendees (which church they attended was not a qualifier for inclusion). The group of church attendees had 50 percent fewer incidences of heart disease, 74 percent fewer cases of cirrhosis, and 56 percent fewer suicides than those who did not go to church.

This study was reported in the Journal of Chronic Diseases in 1972 and funded by the National Institute of Mental Health and the National Heart and Lung Institute. Perhaps because of these studies and others like them, we will find more doctors combining science and the therapies offered by psychology and religion (in its best sense). In addition, these studies and others that will surely follow, can give even more impetus and energy to the religious revival.

Spiritually Incorrect

Who Are the "Spiritually Incorrect?" This group is probably first cousin to the generic Christian and might be considered "spiritually incorrect," by members of mainline churches. The "spiritually incorrect" are those people who, after long years of searching and many pit-falls, begin to live their life in a spiritual way. However, they may not *look like* the stereotype of a religious person. They do not conform to the life style that one typically associates with the religious person. The spiritually incorrect may flaunt standard conventions, and members of mainline churches find this off-putting. It has done my own heart good to see people, who may have been in some way hurt or rejected by mainline religion, find God as a power source in their lives. But this finding of God—or a higher power—has produced some unique individuals. They are unique because the expression of their individual spirituality may appear different than what we are taught as the norm.

Dandy Dan. The spiritually incorrect are "seekers" who have been on a long journey of discovery. Dan Wakefield is a seeker. In a recent article Dan wrote for Modern Maturity, he tells us about his "spiritually incorrect" trek, detailing many twists and turns he has encountered over the years.

As a 48-year-old writer sitting in the doctor's office in Los Angeles, he was told he had a resting pulse rate of 120, about twice what the doctor defined as normal. The doctor asked if he was in the entertainment business. Dan was called to Hollywood to write for Prime Time television and had a great initial few years. After the show on which he worked was not renewed for a second season, he went from studio to studio doing what he calls, "the Hollywood tap dance," trying to get hired as a writer again. It was a long way down for a hotshot novelist who thought his career was made in Los Angeles as a screenwriter.

The doctor said he should try going for a month without drinking. By this time Dan had bought into the myth that great writers are great drinkers. The morning after he had been to the doctor's office, he tells how he woke up screaming. After calming down sufficiently, he pulled a dusty Bible from his bookshelf and read through the Twenty-third Psalm, "...He maketh me to lie down in green pastures; He leadeth me beside the still waters..." He then packed a bag and took the next flight to Boston.

Spiritual anatomy. However, after returning to Boston, Dan Wakefield's life crumbled. A seven-year relationship with a woman he loved ended, he was drinking more, he no longer had his work as a writer, and he was broke for the first time in his life. He attended his father's funeral in May and his mother's six months later.

A distraught Dan was sitting in a bar on Beacon Hill, when another fellow who was a regular there, a house painter named Tony, said he was going to Mass on Christmas Eve. Dan begin thinking about how, at age 11, he had gone to a Baptist Bible school with a friend of his. He'd felt Jesus' presence and had asked to be baptized by full immersion.

On further reflection, Dan decided he wanted to hear some Christmas carols, but not knowing any churches, he located one in The Boston Globe newspaper. Dan writes, "Little did I know that the minister would add some readings between carols, one of them from Helena, an Evelyn Waugh novel about the mother of Constantine, which spoke of 'latecomers' to the manger, and I guiltily thought I'd been fingered, that the message was addressed to me." This prompted Dan to set up a routine of daily exercise, take some yoga classes, and start attending church.

After that church service, and a few more false starts and steps backward, Dan finally found his way to his spiritual path. He began writing and selling again. To everyone's surprise, he also began leading workshops in spiritual autobiography at churches, synagogues, and adult education centers in the United States as well as in Mexico and Northern Ireland.

Some of Dan's friends question why he writes about religion and spirituality. The gist of his reply is that when one writes about a spiritual journey, the words show how God has intervened in one's life as well as show the path ahead.

Many in mainline churches are uncomfortable with Dan, as are some of his old literary writing buddies. "Many in the New York literary world are closet believers," he says, "Seekers who do not want others to know of their interest in God or spirit, for fear it would lower their standing and make them suspect in the world they work in. Though sometimes I get put down from the opposite direction, by holier-than-thou religionists who feel I am too frivolous and worldly to be counted among the elect, I have come to realize that for such ideologues, I am 'spiritually incorrect.'"

Dan feels that God wants us to enjoy life. He explains that, after all, in John 21 Christ appeared after the crucifixion, and when the fishermen were not catching any fish he told them to lower their nets on the other side. "'Come and dine,'" he said to the disciples; " I think he means to the feast of life; I think he means all of us."

The Tank Traps and Mine Fields

<u>What About Cults</u>? In this battle of religions, not all seekers survive as well as "Soul Man" Dan Wakefield, however. Some seekers on their religious journey fall prey to the influence of a cult. Initially, a seeker is drawn into a cult because he is seeking spiritual enlightenment. In the end, however, the person is used to benefit the cult. As Hauck tells us, "The tragedy of the People's Temple in Guyana led by Reverend Jim Jones is an example of unchecked antagonism in the name of religion."

Scott Peck, M.D. suggests a cult would display these identifying characteristics and features:

1) Adulation of the leader 2) A clique or inner circle 3) No checks and balances within the management 4) Hiding of finances 5) Creation of dependency—member must accept "dogma"; independent thought is frowned on 6) Minds are one mind—as if the followers' brains are clones of the leader's 7) They speak as if they have captured God 8) Followers dress alike, look alike, speak alike, although this may be an unconscious rule 9) They usually break-off contact with parents, siblings and friends.

Father Leo Booth's therapy for religious addiction is equally appropriate for treatment of members of a cult and those in cult-like churches. Using the alternative approaches (based on Alcoholics Anonymous), Booth uses these supportive group approaches for the addict's treatment.

Booth outlines the following examples: 1) Instead of thinking in terms of black and white, the addict is encouraged to appreciate that there are "gray" areas of life and one does not always have to have an answer. 2) Obsessive talk about God, prayer, and scriptures and literal interpretation are de-emphasized; attention is focused on the *"spirit"* of the scriptural message. Booth gives this example from scripture: *Wives, submit yourselves to your husbands as to the Lord. For a husband has authority over his wife just as Christ has authority over the church; and Christ is himself the Savior of the Church, his body. And so wives must submit themselves completely to their husbands just as the Church submits itself to Christ. [Eph. 5:22-24]* The treatment goal is toward accepting responsibility for one's life, family and relationships. 3) Refusing to talk, doubt or question is countered by encouraging those very things. 4) The sex is "dirty" attitude is replaced with an approach which helps the person to see the beauty of sex, intimacy and sexuality. 5) Judgmental attitudes and conflicts with science/ schools/hospitals are decreased with knowledge and the various ways God's "spirit" of truth can come through science, medicine and education. 6) Treatment for physical problems—such as back pains, sleeplessness, headaches—are talked about within the whole person concept of the healing of body, mind and emotions, that is to say, the spiritual self.

Balance. One of my closest friends gave me a present for Christmas. It was a polished stone, and on one side of it was engraved the word BALANCE. That was all—just that one word. If we cast any stones at the modern church at all, they should all carry that one word, BALANCE.

Carl Jung's psychological theory speaks about the neurosis that takes over the life of an individual, institution or church when the feminine energy (yin) and masculine energy (yang) are out of balance. When on the seesaw of energy/power, either the feminine or masculine aspect is lowered so as to raise higher the other, this imbalance causes a neurosis to develop. Another way of saying this is when male energy permeates the whole of, say, an institution or event, that energy will be an active, aggressive, power-filled energy. War is an extreme example of the use of the masculine power operating alone without the counterbalance of the feminine. When male and female energy are *balanced* within an institution or event there is evidence of great cooperation, productivity, well-being, and movement to and fulfillment of goals of the group.

Emotional-spiritual balance. The Jesuits' Society of Jesus called for solidarity with women in April of 1995 at their General

Congregation in Rome. When Jesuits speak, people listen. This official statement stunned many.

The 1995 Jesuit statement found that, "systematic discrimination against women" is "embedded within the economic, social, political and even linguistic structures of our societies." And even stronger, "many women …feel that men have been slow to recognize the full humanity of women."

Further, "We have been a part of a civil and ecclesiastical tradition that has offended against women, and," the statement goes on to say, "have often been complicit in the clericalism which has reinforced male domination with an ostensibly divine sanction."

Robert F. Drinan, (a former member of Congress, a law professor at Georgetown University, a legal ethicist and a Jesuit priest) of the Religious News Service, thought the Jesuit statement on women was blunt. But he was proud to be numbered among priests who took a stand on this issue.

Drinan reports the Jesuit Society's premise of "dominance of man" in church and society has barred women from educational opportunities, placed upon their shoulders disproportionate burdens of family life, and limited their access to positions of power in church and in public life.

Many Women Feel Disenfranchised. This has been my own experience at least in my own diocese of the Episcopal Church. Drinan wonders if the fact that there has been a centuries-long alienation of women in the church, is one of the major reasons for the sharp decline in candidates for the priesthood. He asks a convincing question, "If mothers do not feel valued by their church, how can they inspire their sons to become priests?"

To balance (level) the seesaw and heal the neurosis, we see today a rise of the feminine in the most patriarchal of churches. Saint Mary, a highly valued saint in the Church of Rome has been appearing to people all over the world, but in this modern era, only to women and children.

The Jesuit statement urges all Jesuits to listen carefully and courageously to the experience of women. One wonders if members of male dominated churches allow themselves to hear such voices.

How We Develop (Or Not) As Masculine or Feminine

A Roman Catholic Nun Speaks. A number of years ago in Fort Worth, Texas, both a nun and a priest lectured at a Catholic Diocesan Convention. The nun spoke on how the socialization of women influences how they relate to men; the priest spoke on the emotional development of men and how this influences how men relate to women.

The Sister, a psychologist, made a lot of sense to me. She described how the socialization of women, and their subsequent stages of psychological and social development is reflected in their behavior with men in the church—any church. This knowledge is important because the church and its members are better served by recognizing the feminine stages of growth and development. Understanding these stages of development supports spiritual growth and contributes to balance in the ecclesiastical arena.

Stage 1—The woman behaves in a subservient way toward all males, particularly male clergy. She bakes and brings homemade cookies for most meetings, takes their word as law, and does all within her power to be seen in a favorable light by the clergyman in charge. She always concurs with clergy opinions and never asks troublesome questions. She will do all kinds of favors if the person asking is a clergyman. (Taken to the extreme, one woman in this stage provided a female stripper for a Bishop's birthday party....)

Don't get me wrong. Cookie baking and being congenial and helpful is a role played by many fine women in our society. It is easy to see why clergymen would like to have such a "hand servant" about the place. This social activity is fine; however, with Stage 1 women, that is all of who they are. The male in charge, priest or pastor, determines how the women see themselves. They have no self-esteem that is not generated by male approval, in or out of the church. They frown on women who claim to have a calling to become a minister or a priest. In their subservient eyes, only clergymen can act as "God" on earth.

Stage 2—This woman occasionally rears her head and wonders, "What in the world is he thinking?" when she sees a male in authority treat some innocent person cruelly. At this stage, a woman is likely to begin to differentiate her opinions from male opinions on certain issues, although she will seldom speak out loud of these differences. Importantly, there may be times when she owns her own opinions. This means the woman comes to know what *she* thinks and accepts those thoughts and feelings as her own—not something borrowed from an authority figure. Subsequently, she finds she is happier when she connects with her real feelings.

Stage 3—The woman realizes she is a person in her own right. She continues to want to make a contribution to the life of the congregation, but is no longer solely dedicated to pleasing the pastor. She begins to identify with other women who can think independently and who are making progress in helping move the church forward. She has begun to search her own soul and is becoming more connected with a higher power. She is becoming spiritual.

The church and its members are better served by recognizing the stages of masculine development as well. The priest on that day addressed how the emotional/cultural development of men took place in relation to women. He cited three stages:

Stage 1—Baby boys at first are close to their mothers and bond with them. In this stage, the boys are happy to be with their mothers and feel nurtured and protected.. We are now finding that boys, while not so with girls, are made to separate from their mothers far sooner than is good for them. (Recall the work of Pollack in Real Boys and the "boy code" in Chapter 1.)

Stage 2—Especially in adolescence, a boy is made to feel he must separate from his mother. The male faction of the culture wants to socialize him as a male. Often, though, this is done in such a way that the very best part of a boy is lost.

During stage two, the boy disconnects from his mother and his feelings for her. He comes to look upon her and all females as *different*, perhaps even alien. This emotional disconnection results in his being unable to have empathy or understanding for anything female. He may go out on dates, but lust will be his main focus, for how can he "love" someone with whom he has no connection, at any level?

Many marriages today are plagued by the fact that the husband is emotionally disconnected from his wife, and often his children. A stage two man always remains a little hostile and/or sarcastic when in the company of women. He keeps them in their place, and like the King of Siam, his head must always be held higher than her's. (All will be well in this arrangement as long as she is agreeable to keeping her head lower.)

Stage 3—In more fortunate circumstances, a young man may have a series of experiences during which he comes to realize that, in some ways, women think/feel as he does about a subject. As he begins to see that a woman *can* think, he may say to himself, "Wow, she reminds me of Jennie, my favorite sister," Or, "Well, we have a number of issues on which we can agree!" He can, in that way, come to see a woman as more like himself than so very different.   As one male doctoral candidate said to a female friend of mine (also a doctoral candidate), "You're really smart for a girl." With that comment, we knew he was knocking at the door of Stage three!

However, the underlying essence of the yin and yang is, in the final analysis, all about Balance. Here the words of a poet, William Henry Channing, 1898, speak to us about that very theme:

To live content with small means;
To seek elegance rather than luxury,
And refinement rather than fashion; to
Be worthy not respectable, and
Wealthy not rich; to listen to stars and
Birds and babes and sages with an
Open heart; to study hard, think quietly,
Act frankly, talk gently, await
Occasions, hurry never; in a word, to
Let the spiritual, the unbidden and the

Unconscious rise up through the common—
This is my symphony.

Sacred Psychology

Seeing With the Soul. Sacred psychology involves the research of spiritual experiences. It is a psychology concerned with getting beneath the surface of consciousness and helping people to understand the inner map and meaning of their lives. The most gifted of all the psychologists who wrote about the sacred was, of course, Carl Jung. When he was eighty years old , he wrote his life story in Memories, Dreams and Reflections. It includes Jung's sermons collected under the title, VII Sermones ad Mortuos. The book is an unusual autobiography in that it does not tell about any special accomplishments in his worldly life…with the exception of some notes about his work with Freud. His primary focus is on how he came to understand himself in the light of inner happenings.

Jung differed from his teacher Freud about the role of sex in shaping personality. Jung thought that a person's inner religious drives were at least as strong as were his hidden urges. (This means that each individual experiences, at some level of their personality, a longing for a relationship with the divine, and that this longing was as strong as those more basic instincts that went unrecognized by the person's rational conscious mind.)

Morton Kelsey, author of Christo-Psychology, shows us how we can apply Jung's insights to find our own way through the religious maze. He says that Jung, although at first a nonbeliever, went into the vineyard only to explore but returned with some very good grapes for the wine. He is saying that while Jung was at first only a detached researcher of other people's spiritual experiences, in time he not only found valuable insights about the sacred in the lives of his subjects, but he learned about the sacred in his own life. Jung then went on to share the results of his research with others.

Among those who write about the sacred in psychology, my personal favorite writer extant is Jean Houston, a PhD psychologist. Someone once said she is a composite of Rollo May,

Vanessa Redgrave and Billy Graham. She, in her passionate forthright manner, seems to me to be an authentic person with a zeal for her work. Houston has done a prodigious amount of research in the area of sacred psychology. She speaks to the richness of the unity of the sacred with the psychological.

I believe that psychology alone, without the leavening of the spiritual, leaves its adherents in a sterile place. Then, too, spirituality and spiritual growth can only raise us up to the watermark of our own emotional/psychological development.

If one is looking for that point where the sacred and the psychological intersect, it can be found in the life and writings of Jean Houston. There one will see in the cross- hairs of her telescope lens, the intersection of faith and human nature.

Dr. Houston has paid dearly for her teachings. There seems always to be those who will bring down those who would, by their example, enlighten us. She has suffered the attacks of the skeptics and the antagonists alike.

Our greater story. Writing in A Mythic Life, Houston offers powerful soul-changing ways to heal the wasteland in society and ourselves. (Also see The Possible Human.) She also tells us to ask the questions that need to be asked and to re-envision a time of personal loss and tragedy as a potentially transformative event so that a deeper meaning is revealed. In reflecting about Jean's ideas, I wrote the following poem:

Questions From the Stardust Casino

In night's deep swirl
dust flies from lesser stars
the heart looks to places
our eyes cannot

To query mystery's movement
what holds the leaf to stem?
sets sweetness on the lip?

Then something asks
what are we doing here?
what do we intend?

Within the deepening night
what holds the heart in place?
moves it nearer another?

Who of us will live the world's secrets
within our own cosmos?

Whose heart will remember to ask the
questions in which its answers move?

Houston believes in the power of the story, of myth, to
activate society and the individual in transformational journeys to
the healing of self and our culture. She sees no less than the
remaking of society as our principal task.

In her workshop, Jean creates an experience which allows
people to experience the ancient stories. Participants make these
stories their own, and "having walked in the shoes of folks at the
stories edge, we inherit a cache of experience that illuminates and
fortifies our own."

The joining of one's life to great life is a central experience of
what Houston calls sacred stories. These could be the stories of
Eleanor Roosevelt, Gandhi, White Buffalo Woman, the Bible
stories, Deganawidah (creator of the Iroquois League,) Athena,
Emily Dickinson, ancestors or contemporaries, and many others
that have touched our hearts.

Jean Houston writes wisdom like a jazz musician playing riffs.
This wisdom instructs us to develop a rich inner life and to live its
concomitant counterpart in the world. Essentially, she wants us all
to Wake Up!—to know life is best at the feast of cultural and
individual maturity.

Chapter 3 References

Aburdene, Patricia, Megatrends 2010, Hampton Roads, Charlottesville,VA, 2007.

Booth, Father Leo, Breaking the Chains, Understanding Religious Addiction and Religious Abuse, Emmaus Publications, Long Beach, CA, 1989.

Houston, Jean, A Mythic Life, Harper Collins, San Francisco, CA, 1996.

Haugk, Kenneth C., Antagonists in the Church, Augsbury Publishing House, Minneapolis, MN, 1988.

Strickland, Ben and Catherine Geddie, Influence, How to Nurture, Understand, Manage and Enjoy Your Relationships, Bookworks, Fort Worth, TX, 1995

Peck, Scott M., Further Along the Road Less Traveled, The Edited Lectures, Touchstone Books, Simon and Schuster, NY, NY, 1993.

Fowler, James W. Stages of Faith, Harper and Row, San Francisco, CA, 1981.

Jung, Carl, Psychology and Religion, Yale University Press, New Haven, CT, 1938.

Kelsey, Morton T., Christo-Psychology, Crossroad Publishing Co., N.Y, N.Y., 1982.

Wakefield, Dan, "Soul Man," Modern Maturity, Association of Retired Persons, Lakewood, CA, Jan.-Feb. 2000.

Rilke, Rainer Maria, Letters To A Young Poet, Random House, N.Y.N.Y., 1984.

CHAPTER 4: MORALS IN E-COMMERCE

O, what a tangled web we weave, when first we practice to deceive. —Walter Scott

A Presbyterian novelist and preacher, Frederick Buechner speaks of our common ability to share either good or ill as he likens the world to an enormous fragile spider web. "If you touch it anywhere you set the whole thing trembling...As we act with kindness, perhaps, or with indifference or with hostility toward people we meet, we too are setting the great web atremble."

The Harris Poll Election 2000—The State of the Nation, reveals that 78% believe the Economy is in great shape, but only 19% hold a positive view of America's morals and values. We are seeing these percentages reflected in cyber crime on the World Wide Web.

Cons and Chaos on the Web. BBC News reported online in February 2000, that there is a definite problem created by ongoing Internet fraud. They warn e-shoppers to think twice before giving their credit card numbers out to online sites. This word of caution is prompted by the fact that charge card numbers can easily be pirated.

At the international level, Visa officials indicate that half of all their credit card disputes are about Internet transactions. This is the case even though these activities are only 2% of the overall business. Bills are being charged to people's accounts, erroneously, due to credit card thefts.

BBC's Money Program is of the opinion that the huge problem with fraud is due to the carelessness of the banks. But the picture gets even more clouded. Ted Bridis in an AP article from Washington indicated his belief that at least eight days before the February 14th cyber attack on some well-known commercial web sites, the nation's largest financial institutions received detailed warnings of the coming threat to their computer systems and data bases.

Top Secret. Bank officers did not pass on their warnings to the nation's law enforcement agencies for a reason. Apparently participating banks were not allowed to share the warnings with government investigators. It seems there is an uncommon kind of private security network especially set up for banks in this country. Even the location of this security service is highly secret. The idea to have banks protected under the aegis of a security service was brought to fruition by the United States Treasury Department itself. The service precluded giving out any information that let other e-businesses know of the approaching hazard.

Not to be Believed. Even though many e-commerce sites promise security, privacy and protection for the buyer, the public apparently has little belief in such vows. Could it be that our credit cards are no longer going to be the payment of choice for e-commerce? And what system can take its place?

Don't Bite. Those in charge warn us against various scams, exemplified by the following: buying the life insurance policies belonging to people with fatal illnesses. One criminal made $100 million and spent most of it in Las Vegas. The cyber cops report that the dying patients' names were garnered from phone books!

There is also the fraudulent practice of selling shares in companies that do not exist. For example., a page was forged from Bloomberg's financial news website in such a manner as to con others into thinking the price of shares in a company called Pairgain was going up—hence, the price jumped 30% before falling when the forgery was disclosed. Everyone involved lost their money.

Fraud Squads. Hiring international cyber cops to police e-commerce has been proposed. The United States and the United Kingdom are among the countries looking at national cyber-crime police divisions. However, none are up and running as of the last of 1999. Law enforcement agencies are struggling to find solutions to this problem, but they are overwhelmed with the complexity and the wide-spread nature of the crime.

Millipede of the Millennium. And now that the "big deal" has come down—the merger of American Online and Time Warner—will cyber-crime grow larger, too? How will such a huge conglomerate protect itself from attack viruses? There may be no easy answers.

The Feds. A Channel 8 TV News report of February 14, 2000 said that the Federal Trade Commission has received 10,000 reports of fraud. By any measure, 10,000 incidences does seem excessive. Reporters further stated that the Federal Trade Commission suggested payment be made with a credit card—not by check or money order—when buying online. This infers that if the offer proved fraudulent, the bank would not make payment. Of course, as we discussed before, some banks may not be policing these payments. Also, the credit card company might try to get your money back from the sellers. Essentially, then, cyber-bidders beware! Still, it is heartening that Congress has begun to be involved in an attempt to help us out.

Clinton to the Rescue. The Clinton administration is pushing for a bigger budget to cut off computer attacks from anyone, anywhere. Janet Reno, the nation's top law enforcement official, has agreed to request $37 million in additional funds to combat cyber crimes.
The FBI is coordinating an effort to catch the vandals who committed the computer raids that occurred on 2/14/00. These were all out raids on Yahoo! (an Independent Web site,) spreading to Buy.com, eBay, Amazon.com, and Time Warner—CNN.com news site. An online brokerage E-trade Group, a technology news site was also hit.

A Good ol' Stand Off. In spite of these damaging attacks, civil liberties groups are opposing a Federal Intrusion Detective network, or FIDNet, which would act as a kind of "smoke alarm," when cyberspace is being contaminated. Marc Rolenburg, executive director of the Electronic Privacy Information Center, feels this would violate "the spirit of the federal wiretap statue, the plain language of the Federal Privacy Act and the history of the Fourth Amendment." It is my hope that groups will join in becoming part of the solution and not just knots in the problem.

I recommend a cooperative venture because I think this approach stands a chance of ameliorating the situation. As a reminder to these various groups, history bears out that cooperation usually succeeds whereas with combative groups there is rarely a winner.

I was heartened to learn that White House Chief of Staff John Podesta told CNN that in order to make the Internet a safer place to do business, "We need to get together and do what we did to deal with the Y2K crisis." He wisely, in my opinion, feels that the government needs to be concerned not only about business but also with privacy and civil liberty issues. He promised that, "Those issues will be addressed."

Hacker Tacklers. In Berlin on February 14, 2000, in response to the attacks on well known web sites there, German Minister Otto Schily proposed a German task force which would cooperate with United States investigators. What is needed they say are hacker tacklers. Schily and the United Kingdom's Prime Minister, Tony Blair, agree that e-commerce is at the heart of the economic success of their respective nations. Blair says it is his "vision for building a modern, knowledge-driven economy." It is apparent then that e-commerce drives business and thus a nation's economic welfare.

We are Hacked. I can only imagine what a friend of mine must have gone through as she helplessly watched all her business files destroyed right before her eyes...by a computer virus. Opening and destroying someone else's files is not dissimilar to the crime of breaking and entering.

Yesterday an acquaintance told me that upon arriving home from a Superbowl party and turning on her computer, she found a number of acknowledgements of purchases she had made on e-Bay. The only problem was that she had made none of these purchases—amounting to $300,000! She then had to spend time, of course, to contact all the sellers and tell them she must retract those winning bids as someone had stolen her password and had made unauthorized purchases in her name.

Federal anti-hacking statutes call for a maximum of five years for the first offense. Deputy Attorney General Eric Holder thinks these penalties are too soft. But he suggests, too, anyone responsible for a network should install anti-virus tools and do everything possible to counter these attacks.

Internet Ethics and Education. Holder feels that a broader education for young people should be offered continually. He says, "for as yet, they don't feel the same moral apprehension before breaking into another person's computer."

Texas "Rangers." In May, 2000, more than 850 security professionals from around the world met in Austin, Texas for the 4th Annual Economic Crime Summit. Those attending were professionals from both the public and the private sectors. This is the first summit of its kind. The topics included Fraud Prevention for the Elderly, Consumer Frauds, Scams and Schemes, Codes of Conduct, Corporate/Business Due Diligence and what data needs be collected.

Privacy Pirates

Electronic Private Eyes. The general public is asking these questions, "How are we going to respond to our need for privacy when our phone and our computer have "electronic eyes" and stockpile every purchase we make whether in a store or online?" Do businesses have a "moral" code of responsibility toward their customers? In light of these kinds of queries, I think that there needs to be a "legislated" code of morals. New house rules, if you please, for our new home in cyberspace.

Out in the Open. Tennis Hall of Famer, Arthur Ashe said when his HIV was made known to the public, "I just didn't want to go public now because I'm not sick. I wanted to protect the privacy of my family. As of this moment my life is going to change. I will deal with it because I know how to adapt. But it's wearying to have to fight misconceptions and the ignorance that people have about the disease."

So it is that none of us really knows who will have access to our medical records. William Stallings in Protect Your Privacy says, "When you write a personal letter to your doctor, lawyer or lover, do you use a postcard? This question gives me pause. Apparently our private e-mails can be viewed by complete strangers.

Some companies monitor their employees' e-mails through covert access (Cavoukian and Tapscott.) At first blush I thought this sounded like a rather paranoid statement. However, evidence is mounting that businesses are using this kind of surveillance.

Every Life is a Book. I like the humor and cleverness of three sociologists, Ken Lauren, Gary Marx and James Rule who have come up with a "novel" idea. They suggest in a paper by Lawrence Hunter and James B. Rule, "Toward Property Rights in Personal Information," that if you could own your personal information, you could if you so chose, sell the rights to the marketing moguls, or the movies.

Tech writer Simson Garfinkel mentions that owning a personal computer puts each of us at risk of surveillance. When all our personal business becomes public, he deems that there will be a multitude of cyber pirates there to cash in.

Garfinkel has written a new book, Database Nation: The Death of Privacy in the 21st Century. He is so adamant about current and potential abuses that he actually welcomes government legislation to regulate private industry. "Left to its own devices, private industry created a system in the 1960's that was tremendously unfair to private citizens." "Yes," he noted, "there was a free information market, but it was a market in which only business could participate."

A Colleen to the Rescue. Sarah Flannery, age 16, has developed a brand new mathematical procedure for encrypting (hiding a message in code) for Internet communication. This means she has enabled all computer users to make e-mail messages secret. And her code can encrypt a missive in just one minute. This is thirty times faster than it has been done before.

This or something like it may become an avenue which will lead us in the direction of privacy protection. One wonders if this procedure may be used to protect e-commerce and technology as well? Experts say Sarah's code is effective even when high security levels are required. Sarah's code may be the dead bolt we need for the front door of our personal cyber space.

The Shadow Knows. Well, The Shadow and a few million other people know about you and me. Columbia professor Alan Westin, coined the term "our data shadows," to mean we must live up to a new standard of accountability. Garfinkel writes, "And because the information that makes up these shadows is occasionally incorrect, they leave us all vulnerable to punishment or retaliation for action that we did not even commit."

Garfinkel says he is worried that the shadow of our medical records could be abused as well as insurance pricing, lawsuits, and marketers on the Net. With marketers chasing our data shadow about, who knows how business will use or abuse that information.

It seems to me that each of us is continually being called upon to protect our privacy. We make many decisions concerning this each day. Do we screen that phone call and risk offending someone or pick it up and spend time talking to people who want to clean our carpets? Do we e-mail our tax return or do we put it in the mail? Do we list our phone number on our checks? Should we look through the peephole in the door before we decide to answer it? (Yes!) Do we open that e-mail even though we aren't familiar with the sender's address? We make a myriad of decisions every day concerning our privacy.

Picasso Could Paint Without Interruption. But you and I can't turn around without the phone ringing. I personally resent any intrusion into my time. I may be focusing on some aspect of work; writing a paragraph, a poem, a letter, thinking a thought, problem solving.

To be free of intrusions when one needs to work or create is essential. Consequently, I have learned to make decisions accordingly. So, it is not just that intrusions are unpleasant; if they interrupt personal matters, they can destroy productivity or creativity. Nevertheless, private pirates are everywhere.

Still, it is apparent that we are all going to be casting long shadows in the 21st century, whether we wish to or not. And what is that child's verse? You know the one by Robert Louis Stevenson..."I have a little shadow...." The child wonders what use a shadow could possibly be. Well, now we have it. A shadow can be both help and hindrance. But definitely a hindrance if you don't know who is stepping on it!

Garfinkel isn't blind to the blatant abuse the government itself has perpetrated on innocent people in the past. In fact, he makes note of the Japanese people living in the United States who were herded into compounds during World War II. He points out, too, the excesses of J. Edgar Hoover and the FBI. But in modernity, Garfinkel's worse scenario is of the unregulated power of marketers—who know more about us than we know about ourselves.

Garfinkel's notion is not much of a stretch when we are aware that Americans have a propensity to resist solitude and self-reflection. Just today I read in the newspaper yet another article about how many Americans are shutting themselves up with their computers. Artificial intimacy. Norman Nie, a political scientist for Stanford University states a finding from his study, "The more hours people use the Internet, the less time they spend with real human beings." And I would add...the less time they have to think! Reiterating, it is a matter of balance and priorities.

Help is on the Way. Check out what various Internet Web sites offer to help us better control our privacy. Included are:
*Online Guide to Practical Privacy Tools at the Electronic Privacy Information Center (www.epic.org/privacy/toos.html). This program has many good links to encryption programs, anonymous surf services, anonymous e-mail services.
*The Center for Democracy and Technology's data privacy pages (www.cdt.org/privacy/). This will make it easier for you to remove your name from research, marketing and telemarketing databases. (Yes!)
*Junkbusters (www.junkbusters.com). This group has made privacy its business and can pass on good "rules and tools".

*The Direct Marketing Association (www.the~dma.org). This site will answer your questions about marketing groups who are profiling you on their data sheets.

*The Washington Post suggests a book by Beth Givens, The Privacy Rights Handbook: How to Take Control of Your Personal Information. There is a plethora of information about medical records and telemarketing strategies.

*If you wish to be removed from various business mailing lists write to

DMA at Mail Preference Service, Direct Marketing Association, P.O. Box 9008, Farmingdale, N.Y. 11735. Then there is the Telephone Preference Service, Direct Marketing Association, P.O. Box 9014, Farmingdale, N.Y. 11735, if you desire to register as a "do-not-call-me."

*The Federal Trade Commission understands the need for privacy and has brand new regulations about how personal data can be collected. Included in its educational material are facts about identifying theft and online profiling.

The Other Side of the Coin—Too Much "Privacy?"

The Irony of it. There is strong evidence that many of our children feel disconnected and disaffected. It's ironic, don't you agree, that in this age where we are connected electronically in all kinds of way, many kids (and adults too) feel in limbo, left out, "twisting in the wind." Disconnected. They don't feel real. This precipitates all kinds of dangerous fallout. Consequently, some kids can, without compunction, engage in killing their classmates. And although some individuals *have* developed strong relationships over the Internet, this has not cured us of our overall *anomie* in this country...being alone at home and anonymous. If one could interview the computer hackers who have done so much damage on the Internet, one would expect to find they live lives of anomie.

Of course sexual preditors can hide in the privacy that comes with their jobs in various churches, schools and other public institutions. Although because of recent actions by the courts, a spotlight has been shone in their hiding places.

A History of Alienation

Anomie. This word essentially refers to the collapse of social structures governing a group of people. It is also the state of alienation felt by a person. Webster's dictionary defines it as "personal disorganization resulting in unsociable behavior."

Historically, this was the nature of life in Texas. The territory was filling up with strangers without benefit of social structure. I attribute to James Mitchner in his well-researched novel, Texas, the idea that an enormous amount of anomie was present in what was becoming Texas. When newcomers arrived, they thought "the ground" looked level, at first. The territory was really a society in so much flux, it was hard for the new Texans to keep their psychological footing. In the new place everything was different— including values. Many men who came to Texas left wives at home. Houston, Crockett and Travis were among these men. And one of the first laws to be passed in the new nation of Texas forgave bigamy in 1836 if the immigrating male could claim long separation from his legal wife back east. (There is a saying that Texas is hell on horses and women.) Perhaps those women who stayed in the east got the better part of the bargain. Who's to know? However, women are traditionally thought to have a socializing impact on men, and the Texas frontier proved to be a rough and lonely place, greatly in need of their influence.

Walter Who? One of my favorite authors, Larry McMurtry, grew up on an isolated ranch within driving distance of Archer City, Texas. In his book, Walter Benjamin at the Dairy Queen, he reflects on what it is like to be "sixtyish." He also tells about the trauma of living with only a small amount of human contact in semi-isolation for years, until he saved himself by reading books.

I wonder if the "death of my personality" he experienced after his heart surgery may actually have been set in motion in the days of his youth when he was so excruciatingly alone. If any of you have traveled to West Texas, you will understand the feelings engendered by the very long empty stretches of road and the sight of a lone windmill on a vanishing plain. It has been said, one doesn't go to West Texas unless he knows someone out there.

A Good Book. Today, as you may know, McMurtry has gathered his books about him like a fortress...perhaps to ward off the cruel effect of the empty and vast landscape in which he has returned to live. In his bookstore, Booked Up, he has thousands and thousands of volumes. People come to the bookstore from all over the world. And in-between visitors he enjoys sitting in the Dairy Queen in Archer City with the old farmers and matrons sipping coffee—reading and thinking. McMurtry tells us in many ways that everything stems from interactions with other people.

The Biggest and the Best. While one may sense the insecurity that underlies the Texas braggadocio, this characteristic may be a reaction to the intense isolation of the early days. The great distances that one must travel to get from one place to another in the state speak to this. And Texas culture is a newer one than the older more established cultures in the East, hence a little more prone to defending its ways.

It is not my intent to discredit Texas or Texans. I've lived here for forty years and we have raised our children here. I say this because I think the state still struggles with image and continues to experience the historical effects of anomie.

Other Vast Spaces. If a marriage is a business partnership, the couple eventually comes to find that business does not a close relationship make. Although many couples do work together in a business, if they are friends first, the marriage can work.

But many folks have told me they are less alone in a crowd than they are in their marriages. Some feel their spirits are dying there. This is the effect of a relationship void of true intimacy. True intimacy is a relationship in which people feel connected and safe.

Alone in the Crowd. Loneliness and alienation per se were major topics of concern for students studying to be counselors in the '60's. The book, The Lonely Crowd written in the 1950's was saying the same thing then that we are saying 40 years later: People are investing time and energy into things, rather than family relationships. But I can also sense a ground swell of people who are trying not to lose any more children, who want to maintain a stable marriage and who wish to live by and honor their commitment and values. Perhaps the best is yet to come?

A scientist, David Gelernter, gives us another lens through which to view the issue of privacy: "Privacy is a luxury when we can get it. Dignity is really what it is necessary to fight for. And come 2025, life will be better not because of the technology revolution but because of a moral rebirth that is inevitable and far more important."

Chapter 4 References

Garfinkel, Simson, <u>Database Nation:</u> The Death of Privacy in the 21st Century, O'Reilly, NY, NY, 2000.

Stevenson, Robert Louis, <u>A Child's Garden of Verses</u>, Crown Publisher, NY, NY, 1985.

Cavoukian, Ann, PhD, Don Tapscott, <u>Who Knows</u>, Saveguarding your privacy in a networked world, McGraw Hill, NY, NY, 1997.

Stallings, William, <u>Protect Your Privacy</u>, a guide for PGP users, Englewood Cliffs, N.J.: Prentice-Hall, 1995.

Hunter, Lawrence and James B. Rule, "Toward Property Rights in Personal Information," paper presented in the Information and Privacy Commission, Ontario, Dec. 17, 1993.

Riesman, David with Nathan Glazer and Reisel Denny, <u>The Lonely Crowd</u>, Yale University Press, New Haven, CT, 1950.

Michener, James A., <u>Texas</u>, Random House, NY, NY, 1985.

McMurtry, Larry, <u>Walter Benjamin at the Dairy Queen</u>, Simon and Schuster, NY, NY, 1999.

SECTION II: MANNERS

CHAPTER 5: MANNERS IN A WIRED WORLD

Manners are minor morals. —William Paley

Always behave as if nothing had happened no matter what has happened. —Arnold Bennett

The whole field of etiquette is one that nobody wants to practice, but everybody wants others to practice. —Judith Martin a.k.a. Miss Manners

In this section's chapters, all manner of things will be included. Of these essentials, you will find a virtual potpourri of topics promised to ease your path "to the waterfall." This diverse cache of strangely related perceptions are strung on a single thread. In the end you will know the one thread that ties them together.

Lesson From a Fruit Tree. I think it was Joyce Kilmer who said he had never seen a poem as ...well, you know the rest. And then there is another tree lover, H.W. Beecher who said, "People ought to carry themselves in the world as an orange tree would if it could walk up and down in the garden, swinging perfume from every little censer it holds up to the air...."

To carry the "you ought to be an orange" theme a little farther, here is my poem:

Etiquette

Not to discount you,
dear Emily post,
but I for one
prefer another's opinion on
correct social mien

Listen to the poet Sandburg
As he instructs us with these lines:
"Be you like five new oranges
in a wicker basket,
laugh as peaches
in the summer wind."

Sorry, Miss Post,
But he does have a point.

Social I.Q.

If manners are an indicator of your true self and reflect your social I.Q., as some say, then I suppose most of us would want to do the right thing. But we may wonder what *is* the "right thing." I personally like what Jonathan Swift had to say when he remarked, "Good manners is the art of making people easy with whom we converse; whoever makes the fewest persons uneasy, is the best bred person in company."

Conversely, rigid and stiff formal manners may be off-putting or condescending to those who are gathered. As Robert Hall said, "Striking manners are bad manners."

A Big Swig.... I love the story told about Will Rogers on his first "state" visit to Japan. Occasionally, during the elaborate meal prepared in his honor, Will took a big swig out of a bowl by his plate. He noticed that each time he drank from the water bowl, all of his Japanese hosts likewise drank from their bowls. It was only later that someone informed Will that he had been drinking the water in his *fingerbowl*. The Japanese, astute hosts that they were, knew enough to do what was necessary to save their guest embarrassment and loss of face. That's manners with a touch of heart. Give Will's hosts a high score in Social I.Q.

We are not Alone in Our Need to Know. If you try to know what is offensive and try not to do those things, you are in good company. Even the father of our country, George Washington, was concerned about doing that which was mannerly. (And even as he was crossing the Delaware on that fateful night, I can imagine him with certain decorum in his bearing.)

In searching for etiquette rules, young George, it is said, copied down all the rules that he found in a #110 school exercise book owned by the Library of Congress, "Rules of Civility: Decent Behavior in Company and Conversation." And although antiquated, I think we can update the spirit of them (or the few I will list here) to a modern world without straining overly much. Keep in mind that in any era manners are basically about being congenial and respectful. Here is George's list recorded by Mary Rogers of the Fort Worth Star-Telegram:

When in Company, put not your Hands to any Part of the Body, not usually Discovered.

Put not off your Cloths in the presence of Others, nor go out your Chamber half Drest.

Spit not in the Fire, nor Stoop low before it neither Put your Hands into the Flames to warm them, nor Set your Feet upon the Fire especially if there be meat before it.

Shift not yourself in the Sight of Sight of others nor Gnaw your nails.

Kill no Vermin as Fleas, lice ticks &c in the Sight of Others, if you see any filth or thick Spittle put your foot Dexterously upon it if it be upon the Cloths of your Companions, Put if off privately, and if it be upon your own Cloths return Thanks to him who puts it off.

Take no Salt or cut Bread with your Knife Greasy.

Put not another bit into your Mouth til the former be Swallowed let not your Morsels be too big for the Gowls.

Cleanse not your teeth with the Table Cloth Napkin Fork or Knife but if Others do it let it be done wt. A Pick Tooth. And the last one my personal favorite—

Labour to keep alive in your Breast that Little Spark of Celestial fire Called Conscience."

We're Wired

On Constant Alert. As early as 1983, Time magazine was showing some interest in the effects which pocket pagers and mobile phones had on the people who owned them. I was one of the people interviewed (as I had studied stress clinically), and if my calculations are correct that was seventeen years ago. I stand by what I said all those years ago: "I think prolonged use of beepers produces anxiety and probably high blood pressure. And I had never seen anyone respond to a "beep" with a smile or a less than "strident" comment."

Of course, there is a trade off. Our son, a volunteer fireman, relies on a beeper to alert him to an emergency. Also, parents can keep in touch with children and children with their parents. There are many ways they can be used to protect and to facilitate. Many businesses rely on beepers...but 24 hours a day?

But the shocking news, gleaned from that etiquette maven Miss Manners, is that a beeper going off in a social setting is a breach of good manners. There you have it. A breach. You may have noticed that admonition being given more frequently before performances now...please turn off all beepers and cell phones. The suggestion is that one wear a vibrating beeper as a gesture of courtesy to the performers and the audience.

Miss Manners feels if you are on call, it is best not to accept invitations to seated dinners, weddings, or other formal or structured events. Her heart seems to be with the hostess, rather than the on-call guest, saying, "Miss Manners knows how vital your contribution to society is, but you can still get someone to cover for you during your godchild's christening."

Phone Manners

Can't Live With 'em, Can't Live Without 'em. People of my generation (the older generation) and my parents' generation seem to feel they are honor bound to answer a ringing phone. However, I have noticed the younger generation feels no such compulsion. (Though they seem to be compelled to answer each and every e-mail.)

At our house, I am the only one who does not feel it necessary to answer every phone call or e-mail. And I have taken a good bit of criticism for my (occasional) avoidance of picking up a ringing phone. I felt comfortable screening phone calls. But my friends and family have felt my behavior bordered on rudeness. To calm my fears...or not...I went to the source of phone etiquette. I turned to Miss Manners and I am here to tell you, I came away vindicated!

This is what she had to say on the subject. "Screening calls is not itself rude. Even the wildly condemned practice of leaving a machine on at home so that one knows who is calling before deciding to answer *is not rude*. It is no more possible or wise always to accept all calls as they are made than it is to leave one's front door wide open." And continuing the analogy, when the doorbell rings, one doesn't usually fling the door wide open without checking first through the peephole to see who is there. Such behavior is a simple matter of safety in this modern world. Well, there we have it. Thank you, Miss Manners.

And as I have already said elsewhere, the intrusion of a ringing phone leaves me unable to write or think—except in intermittent intervals. It just throws me off-track. It becomes increasingly hard to refocus my attention after a siege of calls, especially if I am doing several things at one time, which is often the case.

I recall working away at my desk and by the time I had fielded six solicitor calls in an hour, I just couldn't handle another intrusion. You may wonder why, if I was so opposed to being interrupted, I kept picking up the phone? It was one of those times when I had asked someone to return my call at his or her convenience. I felt I needed to answer the phone.

The First Clue. My surname is difficult to pronounce so most telephone "spammers" stumble over it. That day when I heard the usual stumble, I just quietly hung up the phone. Immediately the phone rang again. This time I let the answering machine take it. It was the last solicitor calling back, and in a very irritated holier-than-thou voice chastised me with, "Don't you know it is very rude to hang up on people? You should be ashamed of your poor manners."

And perhaps she was right. However, I felt the blame for rudeness should be shared equally. She made the call, as part of her job, but certainly with no consideration as to whether or not I had the time to listen to a sales pitch. Random dialing telephone solicitation is badly in need of a policy or some regulation. Supposedly these callers are not to call after 9:00 P.M. or on Sundays. Someone should tell the people they work for that calling in those "free zone" hours is creating bad will in those of us who need a little relief.

<u>Why Me</u>? You may find this as hard to believe as I do, but the following event actually occurred while I was writing the paragraph above. Our telephone actually rang **five** (count them five) times within **three** minutes! Is this blatant abuse of privacy and the telephone? (Yes!)

<u>Alien Invaders</u>. What do I think is the best and kindest way to rebuff an unwanted caller? I think it best to speak up and get the both of you out of your misery. It is better to be honest and direct than say, letting dinner burn or a good thought slip away because you feel you must stay on the phone to be "nice." You may in all propriety cut in and say, "Thank you, but I'm not interested. Goodby." This short spiel allows you to dodge the "commercial caliber bullet" and you can get on with your life (or what's left of it) and they theirs.

Although telephone solicitors are probably unjustly maligned, they are simply intrusive. For anyone who calls, family and friends included, it is best to set a convenient

time to call or call back. And if you have an answering machine, it is a good idea to say in your recording something to the effect, "Please leave a message and a convenient time for me to return your call."

The telephone should not always have the right-of-way in life's fast lane. Call waiting is considered an abomination by many people, especially those who get put on hold while the other person checks to see who else is calling.

One can sometimes use the answering machine as a bulletin board – a way to exchange messages. Faxes work well in this way too. But a word of caution here. When you send a fax, you never know who else will read it. It is best to treat a fax as you would a postcard. Faxes are basically open communication. No one except the designated recipient should read them, but that doesn't mean they won't be read by anyone else. So write the message with this in mind. Of course the same guidelines are basic to texting. You would not want some confidential message to go astray.

Don't Ask!

A Questionable Question. "What are you doing?" This question ought to be ruled out as an opener for telephone conversations. It affects me in a "catch 22" kind of way. I have to decide if the person really wants to know (not usually).Yet, this very question is asked countless times each day all over the country; probably more often than, "paper or plastic?"

I polled some clever friends of mine to find out how they handle the "questionable question." Most of them have a list of stock answers at their command. For example, when asked the infamous question, they might choose to reply with any of the following: "Husking corn and shelling peas," "Eating bonbons," "More of the same...," "You wouldn't believe me if I told you," and "If I told you, I'd have to kill you."

Of course, if you receive a call at a bad time, you can still be polite by saying, "May I call you back?" without going into the gruesome details. However, if the caller is being cloddish and persists on knowing what you are doing and why you can't talk, repeat yourself. Yes, repeat yourself. But whatever you do, don't go on the defensive about it and prolong the conversation!

How to Get Off the Phone. But what if you've called someone, perhaps a friend, and now you need to terminate the call? Do this in a kind and gentle way with something like, "Well, I guess I'd better let you go now." Or, "I won't keep you." These words let the other person know you are being considerate of their time as well as your own. This manner of getting off the phone is so respectful, it makes one wonder if the Japanese thought of it first.

Cyberspace *is* Society

"Flaming" in cyberspace lexicon connotes sending an insulting message. Not a good practice in cyberspace or in a non-cyber society either for that matter. And "spamming," sending the same message to the masses electronically, is rather like capturing the attention of a large group of people. If it is something you wish to share with others and you think it has value, humor, etc., don't hide the fact you are mass mailing. Be sure you are not coming across like someone waving his arms and hawking his wares at a seated dinner party. Cyber society is, after all, society.

My Father Thanks You; My Mother Thanks You…

<u>And I Thank You</u>. Today many of us are wondering how to send, and if to send acknowledgements of, for example, a congratulatory note. It is best to acknowledge any note of this kind regardless of how the note was sent. The best rule is to respond in kind: that is, to acknowledge receipt of the note by e-mail if it comes that way, or by phone if received by phone. By Pony Express? Well, that's out of my jurisdiction and I will leave you to your own devices!

<u>Poor Form</u>. A form or preprinted thank you is only a cut above sending no thank you at all. A form thank you is O.K. when there are many people to thank and if you insert something into the note that personalizes it.

In her newspaper column, Abigail Van Buren answered a reader's question concerning the correct time limit to send out thank you notes. Here is her reply, "Dear Running Behind: The sooner the better! Certainly no later than a month. And that goes for all gifts—so get moving!

<u>Pushing the Envelope.</u> Contemporary times can present us with some sticklers when we are addressing an envelope to be mailed to an unmarried couple. But Miss Manners clears up the conundrum somewhat by suggesting a tactful way of proceeding.

She says, "Address the envelope only to Mr. or Miss [Ms.]—to the partner you know best and whose name you can spell—inside the card, which is the personal part, address it to "Dear Janet and Charlie." Whew! These things do get tricky.

Teach the Children Well. Parents, here is yet another duty that you must not shirk: teach your children to write thank you notes. Modern day parents seem to have, at times, forgotten this graceful art themselves, but it is imperative that they teach their children the value and importance of this pleasant task.

There are many grandparents out there who have been remembering every birthday, graduation, and special event since the day the child was born. Yet, they may rarely if ever receive thanks. We need to change this! Parents you may unwittingly be teaching your children to see their grandparents as "purses" instead of real generous people. In fact, I know one grandmother who lives some distance from her grandchildren and she calls herself the "purse" grandmother!

Just like required homework, take a few moments, sit down with your child and let them write a due note of thanks. Don't be critical of the writing: let the child write what he or she wants to write. Even if it is something like, "I like the water pistol you sent, especially when I can surprise my dad with it." A handwritten note is always proper and valued. However, if you yourself e-mail your "thank yous", many children can also be taught to express thanks in this way. I've heard that some elementary schools are no longer teaching cursive writing. The times they are achanging.

I hope that E-mail will never replace handwritten notes and letters, for to receive a handwritten missive warms the cockles of the heart. And for the incurably romantic, I include this poem I penned myself about a letter sent in a most unusual way:

Billy's Letter

The wind in the valley
Brings sun to her eye
But she walks all alone
Hears her heart's lonely cry.

For Billy's sweet love
She had sent him a kiss
In a letter all white
Touched red by her lips.

Love's letter though lost
Still stained with the red,
Blew to the treetops
Above poor Billy's bed.

A bird in the morning
Had woven white shreds
A nest in the branches
With a touch of the red.

The fledglings all hatched
Soon flew to the ground
Soft on his blanket
Their cover of down.

Seeing them there
In sunshine's full ray
He awoke as they sang
Her letter that day.

His heart strangely leapt
Before the birds flew
As he saw on their breasts
Her lips' crimson hue.

The wind in the valley
Brings sun to her eye
For Billy has written
She need never cry.

For Billy's sweet love
She will send him a kiss
In a letter all white
Touched red by her lips.

Social Faux Pas: Nonstop Talking

The "Chatty Cathys." Over the years I have spent time in the company of many outstanding women, all of whom have had exemplary qualities. They were intelligent, sometimes decidedly so, thoughtful, humorous, and caring. But, a few of these women had one dreaded fault…they talked "all" the time. Not about silly things, but about all manner of things. In the vernacular, they are known as "motor mouths." I am picking on women here, because I have not met many men who will engage in this particular behavior.

I once heard it said that a person who does all the talking is comparable to a guest who, invited to dinner, proceeds to eat all the food. This type of person is a conversation hog! Surely this would not be considered mannerly in any era.

The language area of the female brain develops faster; before the language area of a male's. While little boys are still making the motor sounds of cars and trucks, girls are making words. I feel there must be more to the problem than brain science. What part does environment play in this?

Mental Torture. For years I have observed in varying situations the effects on the people who were within hearing distance of a "chatty Cathy." Some will get up and leave the room without a word of "excuse me." Other people, who are too polite to cut in or try to change the subject, begin to fidget. I have even seen some instances in which a man developed a hand tremor! Then there were the tortured looks on the faces of the people being "buttonholed." The nonstop talkers, however, seem totally oblivious to the effects on their audience. As a trained professional listener, even I find the verbal barrage taxing to my sensory circuits.

I finally set out to understand the "ear battering" behavior of these women. What drove the motors of these compulsive speakers? Was there something hidden in their background that created the need to constantly verbalize?

In my informal research, I stumbled upon a cluster of variables that I feel might be at least partially responsible for women's compulsive talking. 1) There was either an absent or an alcoholic father 2) The woman as a child often had to make decisions without emotional support 3) There was usually some question as to whether or not they were accepted by one parent or the other 4) They had been put in a position of care-taking as children, caring for an adult—father, mother, grandparent— who was ill 5) The women's somewhat controlled anxiety stemmed from the troubled and or distant relationship between their mother and father 5) Their security and safety needs had not been met as infants 6) Talking appears to have become a way not only to release social anxiety, but to control the behavior of others, while appearing to be social.

The Cry of the Infant. Babies cry to get the attention of adults without whom they cannot survive. In fact an infant's ability to catch and hold a parent's attention is crucial to its survival. It may seem a stretch, but I feel intuitively that their talk is similar to the baby crying in the night. Perhaps these women, for whom a solid sense of self has never developed, only feel they exist, are safe, when someone is paying attention. Their sense of self is lost or fragmented or even totally dependent on having someone validate them by listening to them.

We find in studies of alcoholic families, children are frightened by the silence of parents. For these children it is like waiting for the other shoe to drop. And rather than wait it out, they may instigate problems. They are familiar with chaos. It is as if they are more secure dealing with trouble than with the silence which makes them so apprehensive.

Learning to Tolerate Peace and Silence

Pythagoras way back in 500 B.C. knew human beings were meant to experience silence—and this at a time before the world was wired! We know he valued peace and quiet because he said, "Learn to be silent. Let your quiet mind listen and absorb."

I am frequently tempted to "gift" a nonstop talker—many of whom I wish to keep as friends—with a book called Meditations on Silence by Sister Wendy Beckett. (I will be saying more about Sister Beckett later.) I feel there is such solace in silence. The compulsive talker truly needs help to raise his threshold of tolerance for peace and quiet.

"I Want to be Alone." Greta Garbo said it best and in fewest words, though actually she said, "I want to be *left* alone." And after one's ears have been beaten down listening to a compulsive talker, we understand the almost sinful pleasure in tuning out. Oh, to be left alone! Alone, one no longer owes anyone a response, and there comes the freedom to think your own thoughts.

Because we are all connected in this e-age, thanks to Bill Gates, it behooves us to be sensitive to each other's need for periodic aloneness. Musicians say, "It is the silence between the notes that makes the music."

Towering Babel. Sister Wendy Beckett, a contemplative, does a most unusual thing. She visits art museums to contemplate great art, looking for the insights these pieces offer her. As she viewed "A Tower of Babel,"(c.1563 by Pieter Bruegel the Elder) she saw silence as protective armor against endless chatter. She takes umbrage with words that are misused, "to confound thought, to ward off friendship or attachments, words as occupation." Sister Beckett says these words are a smoke screen. "Babel is profoundly destructive of our energies...To express what one means and to hear what another means: This is a rare thing."

You Have the Right to Remain Silent

Claiming a Space. Though it is a novel idea in our talkative society, the right to remain silent does have merit. In the obvious way, by remaining silent one isn't as likely to reveal one's ignorance. However, by claiming a space for silence we do not forfeit its rewards for some lesser demand. One can literally lose oneself in the endless details of everyday living. As Virginia Wolfe knew, women (and men) need a room of their own.

The space in silence is a rich vacuum that quiets the mind. To be silent is a courtesy you owe yourself. And time and silence are really two great friends that can ease the clamor and chaos. As Sister Wendy Beckett notes, "Silence is making-friends-with-time. Silence does not fight it or waste it; it refuses to run after it. Silence floats free with time, letting the pattern of the moments unfold at its own pace."

Cary Grant Knew. The following prayer was a favorite of the late, great, Cary Grant who died in 1986 at the age of 82. I include it here in its entirety, and although its title is directed at the "aged," *anyone of any age* might find meaning in its words.

Prayer for the Aged

"Lord, thou knowest better than I know myself that I am growing older, and will someday be old.

Keep me from getting talkative, and particularly from the fatal habit of thinking I must say something on every occasion.

Release me from craving to try to straighten out everybody's affairs.

Keep my mind free from the recital of endless details—give me wings to get to the point.

I ask for grace enough to listen to the tales of others' pains. Help me to endure them with patience.

But seal my lips on my own aches and pains—they are increasing, and my love of rehearsing them is becoming sweeter as the years go by.

Teach me the glorious lesson that occasionally it is possible that I may be mistaken.

Keep me reasonably sweet; I do not want to be a saint—some of them are so hard to live with—but a sour old person is one of the crowning works of the devil.

Make me thoughtful, but not moody; helpful, but not bossy. With my vast store of wisdom, it seems a pity not to use it all—but thou knowest, Lord, that I want a few friends at the end." (Author unknown)

Chapter 5 References

Beckett, Sister Wendy, <u>Silence</u>, Dorling Kindersely, London and NY, 1995.

Martin, Judith, <u>Miss Manners' Basic Training</u>, Communication, Crown Publishers, N.Y., N.Y. 1997.

Rogers, Mary, Star-Telegram columnist, Out and About, points from "Rules of Civility and Decent Behavior in Company and Conversation" Library of Congress, <u>www.homeworkcentral</u>.com.

Taylor, Alexander L. (reported by August and Zagorin) "Why So Many Are Going, "Beep," Time magazine, N.Y., N.Y., April 11, 1983.

Van Buren, Abigail, "Dear Abbey," Fort Worth Star-Telegram, Fort Worth, Texas, Feb. 10, 2000.

CHAPTER 6: MARRIAGE MANNERS

The last word is the most dangerous…and the husband and wife should no more fight to get it than they would struggle for the possession of a lighted bombshell. —Douglas Jerrold

A person's character is but half formed till after wedlock. —Charles Simmons

In order to love we must first become lovers. —Harville Hendricks

"Successful forty-five-year-old S.W.M. with private yacht seeks contact with slim twenty-five-year-old S.W.F." This is only a sample of the kinds of personal ads that run in our newspapers each week. The man who posted this ad must have had some confidence that *his* money would attract *her* body. And, indeed, the ad might have resulted in the man's accomplishment of his goal for all we know. After all, he only asked for *contact.*

Marriage, or at least true intimacy, was not part of S.W.M's original plan. Of course, we know men like physically attractive women and women are drawn to successful men. But we also need to keep in mind that when two strangers meet, there can be no intimacy where there is no safety. (Millions of abused women who've made contact without a safety net can attest to this.) Here's what Darva Conger said about being chosen as the bride of a complete stranger on, *Who Wants to Marry a Multimillionaire*? "I wish I had the moral fortitude at that point to walk away. He isn't someone I would normally have chosen as a friend."

While the dream may be to find "immediate intimacy," this is an unrealistic wish. Trust building takes continued contact and step by step, growing to feel safe (physically and emotionally) with the other.

First a couple must work through the age-old power struggle. This is terribly frustrating, because as Harville Hendrix recognizes, "The more you want to be close to each other, the more you seem to fight." This must be the case, as the latest American marriage statistics reveal that 57% of us who marry are divorcing! There is literally an epidemic of divorce spreading around the country. One wonders if this is an indicator of things to come; perhaps a marriage revolution is on its way. The 57% divorce rate and the ensuing angst may mean that in this millennium there may be some alteration of traditional marriage as we have come to know it.

The Marriage Myth. As a marriage therapist, I have frequently found that, after marrying, the bride goes into a state of "marriage shock" and the groom into deep disillusionment. Hence, the marriage myth we are all brought up with (particularly girls): that we will find *the* someone; that special person who will meet our needs, complete us, and we'll live happily ever after."

Belief Cloning. The marriage myth has been replicating itself throughout society for centuries. This belief is the primary parent or cultural culprit that "fakes out" couples married or living together, heterosexual or homosexual, and prevents them from embracing life with each other. The hard truth is that falling in love and "marrying" is no guarantee that the marriage (or relationship) will "take."

As with most things, the cause of divorce is overdetermined. I mean that there is more than one, probably even a number of causes creating this devastating problem. To that end, I determined to put my suggestions for creating a conscious marriage into a letter. The letter is an open letter to all married people, and to those in a committed relationship. Read what is written here as if it were meant for you, take from it anything that helps the spirit of your relationship in any way and leave the rest.

A Love Letter

Dear Anne and Robert,

In the new age our bodies may be full of replaced organs, real and artificial. There may even be someone else's heart beating in your body. Living will be replete with spare parts and spare hearts. Many of us will live to be 100. During this time we will also see all manner of real and artificial couple-pairings in the "marriage market."

Remember the man in Minnesota who advertised for a bride and then let his friends decide which woman he would marry? As a group, his friends interviewed each female applicant. After they selected his bride, the man chose as their wedding site the Mall of America. What were they thinking? But perhaps the groom felt his chances of making a good marriage were as good, going about it in this random fashion, as those who fell in love and then out again.

It looks like from my point on the globe that our lives will be scrambled about in dramatic ways—both in how we live and with whom we live. But our old worries not only about survival, but also how to survive well, will stay with us. Just how does one carry on with all this artificial life? How can we retain our humanity, swimming, as we must, in this turbulent data stream? Looks to me like a lot of traditions will have to be reframed, and revised. But that doesn't mean we have to throw the good out with the bad.

But to continue with instructions to help you in your wish to live in a loving and mannerly way with your beloved:

*As a couple, you don't have to think alike. You don't have to agree on everything, but you do have to <u>think together</u>.

*Learn how to fight without breaking up the furniture, the marriage, the children or each other.

*Don't threaten to leave the marriage when you are upset or have had a bad day—it destroys the foundation of trust that your marriage must have to continue. Threatening to leave the marriage destroys the other person's feeling that you are there for them...that you can be trusted to work on the marriage and get through the hard times. A husband or wife has to feel safe in the marriage or they may look elsewhere.

*Trying to make your partner jealous will backfire. You are both very attractive people (you found each other, didn't you?) and other people may try to "break you up," out of their own spite or envy. Don't help them wreck your relationship to benefit their own ego. Remember, jealousy is comparing yourself with the "competition" and allowing yourself to feel inferior.

*Please, no "game playing." One of the partners may play a game called, "Please Me." Of course, no one can please another all of the time, but it keeps the other trying and failing...finally their heart stops trying.

*The type of person you choose for a partner reflects your own heart.

*You don't owe your parents anything but the 3 C's—Caring, Concern, and Consideration. You don't owe them your life, your happiness, your marriage or grandchildren! You must separate from your parents, and your children must, separate from you— leave home emotionally—or they won't be able to establish their own real marriage.

*Look at each other with "soft eyes." Being critical or having too high expectations for each other kills a marriage and love.

*At times your marriage or your relationship will be more about commitment to each other than it will be about love.

*Keep each other in your private prayers.

*Learn to express and work out your anger constructively in adult ways. If your parents don't handle anger well, you're not stuck with having to handle it like they did—find more productive ways to work it out. (It can be done!) Don't take your frustrations out on each other, your co-workers, kids, the world or other drivers!

*Use "I" statements when conversing about your feelings. Avoid blaming and starting an accusation with, "You didn't..." or "You made me mad." Avoid the "You" word.

*If you have children and if you have unresolved problems in your relationship, the children will automatically begin to have emotional problems. It is highly likely they will act-out the underlying anger in the family. (You can bet on this!) When you have a child who is angry, ongoing, it means you must become more aware of how you handle your own anger and aggressive behavior. A parent with an attitude will soon have a child with an attitude.

*Do you fly off the handle, say aggressive things, threaten, hit, yell, etc.? You are teaching the child that when something doesn't go his/her way or he experiences frustration (a real possibility in the real world), he may do what he has seen you do. However, a different child may go in the other direction and become overly sensitive, cry a lot, maybe even develop ulcers.

*The emotional health of your marriage or partnership will directly impact your children. Also, what you fear will often become what your child fears. What you are confident about your children will, in all likelihood, also feel confident about.

*There is nothing to protect your child from you <u>except</u> your desire to become a mature adult. Desire to learn to <u>love the child in the way that is best for him or her</u>. We often give a child what we didn't get as children, but our children live in a different time and space and may have different needs.

*Know that the best way to protect your children is not by always coming to their defense, though that is sometimes necessary, but by teaching them that certain behaviors have very certain consequences. Many of the men and women in prison have had a parent who never let them experience the consequences of hurting other people. These parents plead with the judge to forgive the penalty for murder! Raising children to become successful adults will be the most challenging, stressful, rewarding, heroic thing you will ever accomplish—along with having a true partner in this life.

*The other person wants to be there for you, but he/she can't save you from yourself. Work at becoming the best person you can be. Learn to confront and handle your own demons. As Sandra Wellborn, President of Waltsan Publishing, says when encountering a problem, the best approach is "Face it, fix it, forget it." Good words!

*Don't ever lose that part of your personality that is kind and gentle, and aware of other people's feelings. In your life up to this point, you have probably overcome many difficult challenges, yet, remember that being both tough and tender is a sterling combination.

*Keep in mind that everyone you meet has, as H. Jackson Brown wrote, lost something, fears something and loves something, just as you have. And we should treat all people with respect, especially those we live with.

*Pay attention to what you say to yourself. If you get down on yourself, you will become depressed or anxious, or hostile—all because of what you are telling yourself! Talk to yourself in ways that are kind and encouraging…just in case no one else remembers to! (These thoughts that cause problems are attached at the end of the chapter for your reference.)

*When you are having family problems, difficulties in the community or at work, or when you feel particularly vulnerable or threatened, problem-solve rather than taking aggressive action. Yes, it is good for you to stand-up for yourself, but this does not mean becoming the aggressor.

*When you argue, don't immediately start defending yourself, or rationalize or intellectualize why you are right. It is better to hear the other person out. Then you can say what you think beginning with an "I" statement. Be truthful about your reasons without being hurtful.

*When you get upset with each other, don't say, "You always…" or "You never…" People aren't that consistent. They don't <u>always</u> do, or <u>never</u> do, anything.

*You may fall in and out of love again and again over the course of a long successful marriage. Expect that sometimes you will love each other and sometimes NOT. It is human nature to need to have some time away from the person you so loved before! But what's really important is that you are each committed to being there for the other person in spirit and in fact. That's commitment.

*A man who is faithful to his wife sets the example for his son to be faithful to his.

*Cut each other some slack. No one is perfect. Not even you.

*Problem-solve together. Something can be done about almost every problem, even if the solution means waiting.

*Pay debts in a timely manner. It is tragic to be buried in debt. It is not wrong to borrow, but have a plan for getting to a place where you can put something aside. <u>Have a battle plan and a time line.</u> Unpredictable things happen, but things can get off track fast without financial goals and a plan; one that you have worked out together.

*Each of you should have some money in your pocket to spend as you please. Then neither of you will feel like a slave. Do not complain about or judge how the other person spends their money.

*Money issues in a partnership or marriage are really more often about power than about money. Sooner or later there will be some problems about money (power). Every couple will need to address these. It is rare for a couple to marry and have the same "money script," or the same ideas about how money is to be conserved and/or spent.

*Life isn't always fair. But for the most part, our life "today" is the result of the **choices** we made each "yesterday". You will never go wrong by choosing to be accepting, thoughtful, friendly, and kind to yourself and others. **Kindness**, even a little bit, will be received like love.

*The effective person doesn't wait until things get really bad or out-of-hand before taking action. Make plans to take care of problems *before* they get serious.

*Learn to play together. Overly serious people are like wet blankets on our emotions. Smile and have fun—why not? **Think joy and laughter**.

*Express your feelings (start with "I," not "You," as I've mentioned before) in a positive way in making a request: "I would feel good/happy/safe/less anxious/etc. if you would spend some time with me when you get home." This as opposed to, "You never spend any time with me."

*Learn to talk to your mate in nonjudgmental ways.

*One person in a relationship should not have to do all the giving.

*Don't gang-up on your mate by pulling in friends or family to side against him/her. As a couple, talk to an objective third party. This should be a person who has proven wise and trustworthy, who will keep your talks confidential and who is not a family member. (Family members may want to be helpful, but they can't always be counted on to be objective.)

*Criticism has killed more love between couples than anything else has. Studies show that saying fewer critical things to your partner, taken along, will raise the level of happiness in your marriage.

*Learn to express yourself. Learn to make requests of each other instead of making demands. Ask for what you want in a direct and positive way.

*Put each other first. Not your parents, not your friends, not your children. A side benefit is that your children will feel more secure and competent as they grow up.

*Neither of you should pair-off with one of the children against your mate. Often, with the birth of the first child, the relationship or marriage ends. This is because the wife, feeling rejected and alone, takes the child as her "love object." The husband, on the other hand, feels he is ostracized, out of the family, and he becomes emotionally separated from his wife.

*Decide to be happy. Make the decision to be happy within yourself. Feel gratitude for even small things. At the end of the day you can almost always find something funny or something to be glad for, i.e., clean sheets, a blue sky, a compliment from a friend, the positive way you dealt with something.

*You are responsible for your own feelings. You are choosing to have those feelings, whatever they are: anger, fear, joy, hurt, etc. Another person can't make you feel any way other than what you choose to feel. We are responsible for our own happiness!

*We drink from our own wells. It is just like that old adage says: what you sow is what you reap. You, to a great extent, are the one who decides how things will play out in your life.

*Remember the only person you need to control is yourself.

*Love sometimes means changing a "bad habit" because it would make your mate happy.

*As the Executive Pair of the family, <u>draw the line</u> with your own family and with your in-laws. This line drawing must happen if you are to have your own marriage, develop your own family unit, rather than becoming a continuation of your parents' marriage.

*Treat your husband, wife, partner better than you treat anyone else—with even more respect than a best friend, a customer or a relative!

*Never attack your mate's masculinity or femininity.

*Don't begrudge your mate having friends or being happy out of your own selfishness or possessiveness. Be happy for their successes. After all, you wouldn't want a mate who has no friends or who isn't successful. Develop friendships in your community with people who are emotionally healthy, or who have a potential for friendship. Do not isolate yourselves as a couple but nourish a growing circle of good friends. It is fine to work hard, but do enjoy a social life together.

*Take special note of each other's birthdays and your wedding anniversary. Some couples also celebrate the day they met. This is the way you tell your partner you are glad they were born.

*When you give something to your mate, you are really giving it to yourself, because what we give is what comes back, eventually. "Giving as receiving" is the heart's way.

*Your relationship with your spouse or mate is really a reflection of how you feel about yourself—if you are happy with yourself, you will tend to be happy with your spouse.

*Take responsibility for your own health and safety – just like you must take responsibility for your own happiness. You can't be much of a parent or a partner if you are not fit. (Notice airlines always instruct parents that in case of an emergency, the adults should put the oxygen masks over their own faces first before placing it over a child's. A parent who is affected can't help the child to survive.)

*What follows are the five phases of most marriages (based on the work of Harville Hendrix's):

1) **Falling into illusion** (You only think you've fallen in love.)

2) **The power struggle** (If a couple can't move out of the power struggle, they either separate or divorce at this phase, only to go back and repeat phase one, sometimes over and over. In this phase, there is an emotional regression and the person's emotional age is somewhere between two and three years of age! But if a person falls in love with someone else—without ever having worked his way through phases one and two, he is doomed to repeat the same mistakes. Elizabeth Taylor has done this eight times! But she should get credit, I suppose, for trying.)

3) **The awareness stage** (One or both of the persons in the coupling realize how to better get their individual needs met rather than to continue to struggle endlessly.)

4) **Learning how to fight fair,** and lastly,

5) **The dawn of acceptance-love** (The other person is accepted as they are with their strengths and limitations. This is love, at long last. And it is what most of us think happens to us in phase one!)

There is an old Indian proverb that says everyone is a house with four rooms—a physical, a mental, an emotional, and a spiritual room. Yet, most people live their lives in only one room. Go into every room every day.

In conclusion, remember this and I promise it will carry the day—

Be a little kinder each day than you have to be.

Yours Truly, I Wish You Love and a Maturing Relationship!

Attachment to Chapter 6

THOUGHTS THAT CAUSE PROBLEMS
(Author unknown)

1. People must love me or I will be miserable.
2. Making mistakes is terrible
3. People should be condemned for their wrongdoing.
4. It is terrible when things go wrong.
5. My emotions can't be controlled.
6. I should be terribly worried about threatening situations.
7. Self-discipline is *too* hard to achieve.
8. I MUST depend on others.
9. My childhood must always affect me.
10. I can't stand the way others act.
11. Every problem has a perfect solution.
12. I should be better than others
13. If others criticize me, I must have done something wrong.
14. I can't change what I think.
15. I should help everyone who needs it.
16. I must never show any weakness.
17. Healthy people don't get upset.
18. There is one true love.
19. I should never hurt anyone.
20. There is a magic cure for my problems.

21. It's others' responsibility to solve my problems.
22. Strong people don't ask for help.
23. I can do things *only* when I'm in the mood.
24. Possible is the same as probable.
25. I am inferior.
26. I am always in the spotlight.
27. People ought to do what I wish.
28. Giving up is always the best policy.
29. I need to be sure to decide.
30. One must always be sure to decide.
31. Change is unnatural.
32. Knowing how my problems started when I was young is essential.

Chapter 6 References

Hendrix, Harville, PhD, <u>Getting the Love You Want</u>, Henry Holt and Co., N.Y.N.Y.,1988.

Komechak, Marilyn Gilbert, PhD, <u>Getting Yourself Together</u>, cdBooks ™, Waltsan Publishing, Fort Worth, Texas, 2000, ebook and paper edition, Amazon.com 2013.

CHAPTER 7: THE MOUNT MCKINLEY OF MANNERS TOLERANCE AND FORGIVENESS

The responsibility for tolerance lies with those who have the wider vision. —George Eliot

Two points of danger beset humankind; namely, making sin seem either too large or too small. —Mary Baker Eddy

Tolerance comes with age. I see no fault committed that I myself could not have committed at some time other. —Goethe

Mental health is the disposition to find good everywhere. —Waldo Emerson

Not by Chance. The entire world is aware of Japan's excellent technology and proficient skill in producing high quality manufactured merchandise. But as Naisbitt and Aburdene tersely comment, "It is not by chance that the United States has 188 Nobel prizewinners and Japan has 5."

A "Tolerable" Mix. The greatest advantage that the United States has over other countries is that it has become the dwelling place of a great ethnic mix of peoples. Because it is one big kettle of hybridized citizens, the United States has been given a creative "leg-up" in competition in the world's economy. Japan was, as you recall, a closed society for so much of its history. She may have been able to control the kinds of citizens produced and to preserve ancient traditions which made life in that country more comfortable, more homogeneous, but other qualities may have been slighted. The Japanese note the creativity that abounds in our country and inquire into our processes, wondering how they might become more imaginative.

Golden Egg in Harm's Way. America's multicultural population, spawned by cultural diversity, is enriched in all the elements that cause it, in many ways, to be the best place in the world to live. However, hate crimes are on the verge of "killing the goose that laid the golden egg"…and, subsequently, every valuable thing we have in this country. After all, hate crimes are violence done to someone who is "different than" (unique from) what is thought of as "the majority of people" or the norm in some way.

Texas as a Macrocosm

Braggin' Rights. Having lived in Texas now for forty years, I am quite familiar with how proud Texans are of Texas. But sometimes Texans can be downright insulting. For example, the old Texas saying, "The cowards never started, and the weak died on the way," may not set well with those in other states. I can well imagine how it "tweaked" the state pride of other people as they migrated westward (often under great hardship) to hear the Texans' song of braggadocio sung to the tune of "America":

> There are no flies on us,
> There are no flies on us…
> No flies
> There may be one or two
> Great big green flies on you…
> There are no flies on us,
> No flies on us…

You're O.K. if You're Family. We never tire, though, of hearing the stories of the Alamo and all the glory of the early days, as we bask in the glow of Houston's Manned Space Flight Center. But while Texas is geographically very diverse, having many different kinds of topography and terrain, Texans tend to possess (in varying degrees by individual) the same habit the rest of America's Americans possess: the habit of boasting about ancestors but complaining about, often being intolerant of, the current immigrants.

I think it helps our image to have singer/songwriters like Lyle Lovett around to sing his welcoming song, "Texas Wants You Any Way." Lyle's song helps dissolve the old line drawn in the dust when Texas first came into the Union. Although part of the union, it still thought it was a country unto itself. The words of the song tell you that we want you to come join us—we know you're not a native Texan, but we welcome you. Soon you will be calling Texas your home and us your friends. If the directors of the various Chambers of Commerce in Texas were alert, they would be playing that song from all the loudspeakers at all their rallies!

And, yes, there are problems with people crossing over borders without passports and "coyotes" (lawyers) making money helping Hispanic people cross. Most dangerous of all are the drug corridors from Mexico into the United States. Both countries lose when these predators are allowed to ply their wares and evade capture. There are some terribly negative ways this impacts the people and the economy in the United States. But in so many other ways, for example, the Latino influence has helped Texas and the rest of the country.

Tortilla Wall. If one were to explore the history of Ozona, Texas, (the only town in Crockett County) with an eye toward medieval world history, the early days of that county look rather much like a feudal society. True, there were no castles, knights or serfs as described in ancient texts, yet the way the great land owners (ranchers) used Mexican hands ("peons") to work the ranch still exists today. The people of Mexico were used to working on the *haciendas*, the great estates of wealthy landowners. It must have seemed very much like the same system to them, just in Texas across the border. While there is a definite social division firmly in place today, (which the Mexican-Americans seem to prefer as much as the Anglos) there is a solid interlacing of the two cultures. Most civic organizations and professional groups in Ozona are a mix of the Hispanic and the Anglo. Most Anglo ranchers in Crockett County can speak ranch Spanish and the Latino folks sprinkle their speech liberally with "Tex-Mex."

Though it has its social critics, a better term for Ozona's economic lifestyle may be *Hidalgo*. Allan R. Bosworth an early resident of Ozona said, "Maybe one should say that it is run on the *hidalgo* system. Hidalgo is a Spanish contraction of *hijo de algo*, meaning a son (of a man) of property." This is because almost all the land owned by the early ranchers has been handed down and is today owned by their sons and daughters. In that sense it is a semi-closed economic/social society.

Border Guards. "Bill Jordan is a Border Patrolman stationed down at Port Isabel, and maybe you've seen him on TV. Bill is six feet, six inches. He can hold a Coca-Cola bottle at arm's length, drop it, draw his gun, and shoot it to splinters before it hits the ground." (Quote from J.W. Holland, former San Antonio District Director of the United States Border Patrol.) Bill's job, indeed the job of all border guards, is to guard along the wild 889-mile Texas bank of the Rio Grande from Port Isabel to El Paso. He is looking for a composite man who Allan Bosworth calls, "Juan Garcia." I quote, "Juan is a Mexican 'wetback' - an alien who wades or swims the border river to look for a job that will earn him solid *Yanqui* dollars. Sometimes he is barefoot and has a piece of rope holding up his pants; always he is hungry. Despite his lowly status, however, Juan has played a considerable role in the economic and sociological development of Crockett County, and has been one of the most controversial figures to appear in Texas since the days of the Governors Ferguson—Jim and 'Ma'".

What Would I Do? I have listened to more than one border guard express his personal feelings when asked what he would do if he were in the shoes of a "Juan Garcia." One guard expressed a sentiment held similarly by many. "If I were a Mexican man and my children, my family, was starving, I would be doing the same thing he is doing...trying to go some place where I could get a job. I'd be crossing the border to make some money to buy food and clothes for them."

A song by Texas son and singer/songwriter Robert Earl Keene, called "Mariano" tells a story with a similar theme. I wrote the following song lyrics with Dwayne Allison, D.O., as a way to give a voice to those who are living a desperate existence and have no voice. As you read these words, you may recall your ancestors, too, crossed water, were often unwelcome, and were the "strangers in a strange land." Poet Stephen Vincent Benet wrote, "...When you say, 'I will have none of...this stranger. You have denied America....'"

Tortilla Wall © 1995

They found Rodriquo west of El Paso, there was no place left for him to hide

They dragged him 'cross the sand, there in the bad land, said it's time for you to take a ride

Oldest in his family he swam the Rio Grande, some things he will never tell.

Hadn't heard of the Iron Curtain, but he's battered and hurtin', while they're starvin' down in San Miguel. His hopes turned to fears and scattered like tears left to dry in the west Texas sun

And, he could see by the gazes of the other sad faces he wasn't the only one

But, he knew in advance he was takin' a chance, prayin' for a change of luck. And for all of his schemin', hopin' and dreamin', he's headed back in the back of a truck.

Chorus

Rodrigo, he's like me and like you, where can he go, and what else can he do

He say, I'm no gringo, but I'm not what I seem, we are amigos chasin' the same
dream

He's just a man and as anyone could tell, he's no Pancho Villa at all

If they could just understand that it's harder than hell, breakin' through Tortilla Wall

Workin' hard as he can washin' cars for the man in downtown San Antone

And it's been almost a year since he made it back to here, sometimes he thinks
about goin' home

A senorita pulls in, in her Mercedes Benz, and he looks as long as he dares

But, each pay day he knows that his money all goes, *con corino* to his family down there

Chorus   Repeat

Bridge
And if he ever gets to heaven, he won't need no green card
He'll have his own Mercedes Benz, there'll be no coyotes or border guards

Chorus   Repeat

The Border as a Metaphor. We have a peaceful but sometimes sticky relationship with Canada on our northern border and a love-hate relationship with Mexico on our southern border. Historically, borders are places where many people and things are funneled into a few narrow crossings. Borders are traditionally places where confrontation is always a possibility. But in this new millennium, perhaps we can imagine *borders as fascinating places that can be re-imagined* for the future.

What takes place at and on borders between countries is reflective of many things. Paramount among them is the gem, sometimes hidden, of the possibility of symbiotic, productive cooperation. But that will take tolerance. And one could say that tolerance is simply a younger form of mercy.

The Colors of a Culture

Multicolored Society. The editors of Megatrends 2000, forecast that our multicultural society will continue to merge. And with that merging we will see a wider variety of skin colors. "There will be more interracial marriages every year. In a hundred years the countries' population will be nonwhite—many folks will be a soft shade of mocha."(Or ochre?) Of course, the challenge to us as a democracy is, will we be able to tolerate all the various shades of people we are becoming? (The editors of <u>Megatrends</u> aren't saying it should or shouldn't happen; they are saying it is happening and will continue to happen.) Considering this prediction, in a hundred years tanning beds will be an unknown or at best a curiosity.

    <u>The Color of a Spirit</u>. Just as John Brown committed himself to freeing the slaves, and died a martyr, an ex-slave left a spiritual legacy to an affluent white Episcopal Church. Her name was Lisette Denison Forth and she has been dead for 133 years. When she died, she gave all of her savings and property for the establishment of an Episcopal chapel. The church, Grosse Ile's St. James' Church marked its 130th anniversary in 1998 and paid homage to the woman who raised the children and cooked for the Biddle family in Wyandotte, Michigan. "It's incredible that she would do all of this for us, especially considering Blacks didn't even live on Grosse Ile…and considering what was happening to her race at the time."

    Lisette, in my mind, did a great thing providing the means for a chapel to be built for the white people. And, who knows… perhaps she has helped save a few white souls in the mean-time. She was similar in her intentions to John Brown—only in a gentler kinder body.

To Do Something Real in the World

    <u>The Unexamined Life</u>. I quote here from Carl Jung to help explicate certain of the inner dynamics of prejudice and intolerance. "We can be convinced that certain people have all the bad qualities we do not know in ourselves or that they live all those vices which could, of course, never be our own." He goes on to warn, "We must still be exceedingly careful in order not to project our own shadow too shamelessly." To project is to cast what we do not own in ourselves onto someone else. Or a group of "someone else's." Hence, racial hatred—actually unfounded hatred of any kind.

    "But if a person sees his own shadow, his own projections, and knows that what is wrong in the world is wrong within him or herself, <u>and deals with it</u>, that person has done something real for the world."

Jung feels that no one can see a thing in a real way if he can't see himself. For, when we do not know ourselves inwardly, we are doomed to bring along all our unconscious baggage and dump it into all we do.

Tell it Like it is

<u>Agents of Intolerance</u>. John McCain, Arizona senator and presidential candidate, spoke in Virginia Beach, VA on February 28, 2000. He prefaced his remarks about the religious right of the Republican Party by saying that he holds conservative views himself. From there he went on to a scalding rebuke of the Christian conservatives, calling them "agents of intolerance." McCain said in his address that "The political tactics of division and slander are not our values. They are corrupting influences on religion and politics, and those who practice them in the name of religion or in the name of the Republican Party or in the name of America shame our faith, our party and our country."

The Sexual Political Refugees

<u>No Tolerance</u>. Like the road sign markers warning passing drivers that NO amount of speeding will be tolerated, many gay people live in a society where there is no tolerance for them and their lifestyle. They are subjected to violence and humiliation and live in fear of their lives everyday. The lack of tolerance has created sexual political refugees, who fear they cannot safely exist in our society.

Morton Kelsey, psychologist, minister and pastoral counselor, quotes Dr. Blanche Baker on the topic of homosexuality. Dr. Baker, a therapist, has done a great deal of work with gay people in her practice and says, "I do not look upon homosexuality as a neurotic pattern. Just as some people prefer blondes and others brunettes, I think that the fact that a given person may prefer the love of the same sex is his or her personal business. But a neurosis can develop because society was so hostile to them, their families often do not understand them, so they are subjected to a great many pressures and a great deal of unhappiness."

Many professionals in the field of psychology and psychiatry have concluded that, basically, homosexuality is not a moral question. Like Dr. Baker, many of them feel that, with the exception of some African-Americans in certain sections of the South, gays in our population are the most rejected and cut off from normal social life.

Mary Baker Eddy, Christian Scientist leader, declared to her followers that, "Two points of danger beset humankind, namely, making sin seem either too large or too small." And some very vocal people in our country have made overmuch of homosexuality. They have wrapped it around with disgust and rejection.

John Bosworth in his book, Christianity, Social Tolerance and Homosexuality, notes that the early Church was not violent in regard to homosexuality. Yet, by the 13th century, witches were being burned at the stake along with heretics. The church was busy fighting infidels and banishing usurers. Boswell reports that Greeks had no word meaning homosexual and that many of the New Testament words translated as homosexual refer to a male prostitute.

In the New Testament, homosexuality is not singled out; Paul made the point that anyone who is touched by any vice has not the right to criticize or judge his or her brothers or sisters. "Judge not lest you be judged."

Father Leo Booth writes, "Homophobia is a result of religious addiction when the addict sees homosexuality as a deadly sin. When this person has a homosexual feeling, he experiences a barrage of enormous guilt and shame which is then projected outward as 'hating gays.'" Psychologists believe that feelings which are denied expression tend to be those which are feared in the extreme. Marilyn Vos Savant, columnist for Parade magazine, writes that instead of spending time and energy "straightening out" the homophobic, we should be teaching the society at large the value of tolerance and the heartbreak of intolerance.

Religious scholars continue to emphasize that there is nothing in the teachings of Christ to foster the violence and rejection to which homosexuals are subjected. In the early days of monasticism, "sex" was considered an evil thing. However, many modern day churches teach that when there is a spirit of love between responsible couples, sex can be a fine and beautiful thing that ties people together in affectionate bonds. (This is not the same as saying that sex used to avoid relationship—as it can be—is condoned.)

A tract, "Toward a Quaker View of Sex," published by the Friends' Home Service Committee in England, offered that sex can be used not only for procreation but for the loving bonds it creates within the hearts of the couples.

There are of course sick heterosexuals and sick homosexuals. Those individuals should be subject to the rules that protect public decency, minors and others who have no right to consent. Mental illness is not selective on the basis of sexual orientation. One psychiatrist said that homosexuality is no more a matter of morals than a peptic ulcer.

Many people in the field of human development, psychology and sociology know that human beings are bisexual, and a few of us are at the extremes—totally homosexual or totally heterosexual. Our sexual feelings are stretched along a many-pointed continuum as Morton Kelsey and others point out.

Stranger at the Gate

Mel White was a ghostwriter for the autobiographies of tel-evangelists Pat Robertson, Jerry Falwell and Billy Graham. In a 1998 speech at an Indiana's Brethren school, Manchester College, Mel talked on non-violence. He said he fell in love with a boy at age thirteen and spent the next 35 years trying to get cured. He even underwent electroshock therapy.

"Much rhetoric," he noted, "focuses on sex, which is not what homosexuality is about. Sex is an extremely minor part of our lives. It is about feeling comfortable, loved and safe."

"It is up to every person to embrace non-violence in their lives, no matter where they stand on the homosexual issue." Mel told of the fear that gays live with, as illustrated by the savage beating death of Wyoming student Gary Shepherd in the fall of 1998.

Mel White is a loving father and grandfather. He is also the minister of a very large Dallas, Texas congregation of gays and lesbians...one so large the Ku Klux Klan drapes themselves and annually attends a service in protest. Mel says, "Jesus loved the outcasts. The scriptures thought to condemn homosexuality are taken out of context and are not accurate historically. Jesus never spoke about the issue and only talked of love, not condemnation."

They Would Turn Cinderella Into a Pumpkin. It is not hard to see that the Religious right does not wish to extend their Christianity to gays. You will recall a recent episode in which the Christian right was reportedly boycotting Disney movies. And yes, a few of the films did have passages unsuitable for children, but they were not the mindless violence we often see as entertainment.

Molly Ivins, columnist for the Fort Worth, Texas, Star-Telegram expresses this thought, "The Christian right's real problem is not Miramax movies but gay people. Disney's health insurance programs for its employees cover the "domestic partners" of gay employees." Hitler scapegoated the Jews. Don't let us in this country be guilty of scapegoating our homosexual population.

Teach Tolerance. Marilyn Vos Savant (Parade columnist) gives her answer to a question about the origin or "cause" of homosexuality —is it choice or genetic predisposition? She responded that if we think gay behavior comes from a single source, we may be operating on a false premise. She says, "In short, I think some people are neurotic because they're gay (and straight people drive them crazy), and some people are gay because they're neurotic (and these people drive everyone crazy). But most are perfectly fine. And just as good as the rest of us. Michelangelo, Leonardo da Vinci, Julius Caesar and Alexander the Great—the military leader who conquered the known world—all were homosexual to some extent. How much more proof could we need that gay people are worthy of respect?"

Tolerance then is also a kind of good citizenship. It is a merciful kindness that is willing to accept another person with all their "differences." With tolerance being the driving power, we can work together for the betterment of us all.

Forgiveness

The Realpolitik. One of the best comments about forgiveness I have read is a quote from Archbishop Desmond Tutu in Parade. Remember, he has lived through the evils of apartheid and now heads a commission to reconcile the former victims and oppressors: "Forgiveness is not nebulous, unpractical and idealistic. It is thoroughly realistic. It is realpolitik in the long run. We in South Africa do not have a blue print, but we have understood this lesson. Ultimately you discover that **without forgiveness there is no future.**"

What it Isn't. This isn't easy. Forgiving someone is not saying, "I forgive you." And it may be one of the hardest things for a human being to do. To be able to forgive is at the top of the list of mature spiritual forms. When we unpack it, we find it is made up of compassion and empathy.

Pargament and Rye, in Dimensions of Forgiveness, say that to let go of justified anger and hurt, and to give up the right to strike back calls for change within us at many levels: we have to change the way we think, the way we feel, our logic, the desire for revenge, our will and our spirit! But in forgiving there are many benefits for the forgiver. Forgiving bolsters physical as well as mental health.

Stress Hormones. A grudge is a commitment to remain angry. But this releases stress hormones into the blood stream and there is a lessening of the effectiveness of the person's immune system. Some scientists believe there is a psychoneuroimmunology of forgiveness. Forgiveness reduces chronic and acute anger. It can also reduce heart attacks and lower blood pressure. Resentment, however, is poisonous. Resentment diminishes and eats away at the self. To forgive offers you peace and happiness.

An Eye for an Eye. Retaliation of the same degree as the transgression can cause a major problem. Think about this. If you hurt someone back to make them feel the hurt as much as you felt—called getting even—the perpetrator becomes the victim and you are now the offender. (The code of the west was that if you lived by the gun you died by the gun.) Definitely a no-win situation. Not that one shouldn't be able to stand up for oneself; defend oneself and one's dignity if necessary. But getting even is a double-edged sword. And Louis B. Smedes said, "Vengeance is almost always frustrated."

Know How to Rescue Your Relationships. There is so much conflict and thoughtlessness between partners in our homes. This often escalates just before the marriage ends. The fact that more than half of the marriages in this country end in divorce is reason enough for all people to learn to embrace tolerance and forgiveness. There are genuine ways to heal personal damage for the benefit of our relationships and for the most vulnerable, our children. Everett Worthington gives us a Pyramid Model of Forgiveness. It has five steps:
1. Recall the hurt
2. Empathize with the one who hurt you
3. Give the altruistic gift of forgiveness
4. Commitment to forgive
5. Hold onto the forgiveness

Hope Yes, Reconcile, Maybe. Forgiving someone does not mean you give him or her another chance to hurt you all over again. You may not re-establish a close relationship where you have to take them out to lunch. Reconciliation is good, very good. But reunion is not always possible, and it has been said, sometimes, cool coexistence is the best it is going to be.

It always helps me in understanding others to realize that, if I had been born in those circumstances, with that body and with their experiences, I would be acting very much like that person. This helps to re-frame my perspective and puts the betrayer and the betrayal in a new light.

I will leave you with this list which in the course of my practice I shared with many people, including the professional religious. I also benefit from the review.

HOW TO FORGIVE
(Author unknown)

The art of forgiving is one of the most advanced spiritual graces. A few simple suggestions are:

1.   Begin by assuring yourself that you have not been seriously injured after all.

2.   Count up all the favors and kindness that have been shown you even by the person who has injured you.

3.   Begin to list the undeserved mercies you have enjoyed at the hand of God.

4.   Offer thanks to God for the spirit of forgiveness with which God has followed you.

5.   Offer an honest prayer in behalf of the one who has wronged you.

6.   Look for some opportunity to help the one by whom you have been wronged.

7.   Surprise him/her with some act of service.

8.   When the memory of your injury intrudes upon you, match it with a kindly thought or deed.

9.   If the wrong is particularly acute, before falling asleep at night, enfold the memory thereof with prayer.

10.   Repeat slowly and carefully the phrase from the Lord's Prayer: "Forgive us our trespasses as we forgive those who trespass against us."

11.   Whatever you dislike in another person, to be sure to correct in yourself!

Chapter 7 References

Naisbitt, John and Patricia Aburdene, <u>Megatrends 2000</u>, Avon Books, N.Y.N.Y., 1990.

Krodel, Beth, "Ex-Slave's Spiritual Legacy," The Anglican Digest, Vol. 41, No.1, Published by SPEAK, Eureka Springs, Arkansas, Lent, 1999.

Bosworth, John, <u>Christianity, Social Tolerance, and Homosexuality</u>, University of Chicago Press, 1980.

Bosworth, Allan R., <u>Ozona Country</u>, Harper & Row, N.Y.N.Y., 1964.

Benet, Stephen Vincent, <u>Western Star</u>, Farrar and Rinehart, Inc. N.Y.N.Y., 1943.

Jung, Carl, <u>Religion and Psychology</u>, Yale University Press, New Haven, CT., 1938.

Hutcheson, Ron, "McCain speech assails religious right leaders," speech reported to Fort Worth, TX, Star-Telegram, February 29, 2000.

Kelsey, Morton T. PhD, <u>Prophetic Ministry</u>, The Psychological and Spirituality of Pastoral Care, Crossroads, N.Y.N.Y., 1984.

Booth, Fr. Leo, <u>Breaking the Chains</u>, Understanding Religious Addiction and Religious Abuse, Emmaus Publications, Long Beach, CA, 1989.

White, Mel, "Standing at the Gate," speech given at Manchester College, IN.

N. Manchester, IN, for Peace Studies Program sponsored by the college and the Brethren Church. Reported by Worth Weller, November, 1998.

Vos Savant, Marilyn, "Ask Marilyn" <u>Parade</u> Magazine, Parade Publication, 711 Third Ave, N.Y.N.Y., March 31, 1996.

Worthington, Everett L., <u>Dimensions of Forgiveness</u>, Psychological Research and Theological Perspectives, Templeton Foundation Press, Radnor Pennsylvania, 1998.

Pargament, Kenneth I. and Mark S. Rye, "Forgiveness As a Method of Religious Coping," in <u>Dimensions of Forgiveness</u>, Ed. Everett L. Worthington, Templeton Foundation Press, Radnor Pennsylvania, 1998.

Greer, Colin, "Without Forgiveness, There is No Future." A report of Archbishop Desmond Tutu's response to a Truth and Reconciliation's report on five decades of human-rights abuse, for <u>Parade</u> magazine, Parade Publications, 711 Third Ave., N.Y.N.Y., Jan. 11, 1998.

ABOUT THE AUTHOR

Before working twenty years as a licensed psychologist and therapist in private practice in Fort Worth, Texas, Marilyn Gilbert Komechak was on the staff of the Fort Worth Child Study Center, and was the Associate Director of the Center for Behavioral Studies at the University of North Texas. She holds degrees from Purdue, Texas Christian University and her Doctorate from the University of North Texas.

During her work as a psychologist, she also served as a consultant to schools, businesses, and corporations. She had ten articles published in various professional journals. While maintaining her private practice office, she wrote a self-help book, *Getting Yourself Together*. The CD-ROM edition was introduced at the Chicago Book Expo by Waltsan Publishing.

A second book, also published by Waltsan, *Morals and Manners for the Millennium*, was presented at the Austin Book Fair. She is a prize-winning poet and short story writer. Her poetry and short stories have been published in the U. S., Canada and Europe. Her children's book, *Paisano Pete: Snake-killer Bird,* published by Eakin Press of Austin, garnered the Oklahoma Writers' Federation, Inc. [OWFI] "Best Juvenile Book of 2003". Marilyn has participated in numerous readings and book signings in Texas. The book, *Deborah Sampson: The Girl Who Went to War*, has been well received by a readers' review panel that passed the book with high marks.

She is a member of Fort Worth Writers, the Fort Worth Poetry Society, the Poetry Society of Texas, the Fort Worth Texas Songwriters' Association, Tuesday Study Group Trinity Episcopal Church, *Who's Who of American Women*, and *Who's Who in America*.

OTHER BOOKS BY THIS AUTHOR

Getting Yourself Together, 3rd edition, available Spring, 2013, Amazon.com.

Tales from the Bumpity Road, available Spring, 2013, Amazon.com.

Deborah Sampson: The Girl Who Went to War, 2012, Amazon.com.

Paisano Pete: Snake-killer Bird, Eakin Press, Waco, TX, 2003.

Fiction Poetry Memoir & More, Fort Worth Writers' Anthology, includes short stories, memoir and poetry by Marilyn Komechak, available Spring, 2013, Amazon.com.

SHORT STORIES BY THIS AUTHOR

The Redneck Review of Literature, "The Well Full of Wishes," No.15, Fall, Twin Falls, Idaho, 1988.

New Texas 2001, "Just One Good Thing," University of Mary Hardin-Baylor, Belton, Tx, 2002.

The Judy and A.C. Greene Literary Festival Anthology," The Parlor" , sponsored by The National Endowment for the Arts, the Writers League of Texas, Texas Commission on the Arts, Salado, TX, 2002.

Suddenly V, "Target Practice" (Christmas Eve in West Texas), Stone River Press, Houston, Texas 2003.

Aries 2003, "The Price of Red Carnations," Texas Wesleyan University, Fort Worth, TX.

Voices of the Heartland, "Camping Out" (a variation), William Bernhardt, Hawk Publishing Group, Tulsa, Oklahoma, May, 2005.

Aries 2005, "Thunder in February," Texas Wesleyan University, Fort Worth, TX, July, 2005.

Westview 2009, "The Whole Enchilada", Spring/Summer issue, Western Oklahoma University, Weatherford, Oklahoma.

Made in the USA
Charleston, SC
16 April 2015